"Dr. Rapee and his colleagues combine the best of recent research and their considerable clinical wisdom into a state-of-the-art approach to treating anxious children and adolescents. For those new to the treatment of anxiety disorders, the book presents an exceptionally rich introduction to the field. For the experienced clinician or researcher, the authors provide a panoply of clinical pearls that differentiate the expert from the merely good clinician. The chapter on applying basic child management skills is itself worth the price of the book. A masterful and marvelous addition to the literature, this book should occupy a prominent place in the library of anyone who treats or teaches others how to treat anxious youth."

—John S. March, M.D., M.P.H., Programs
in Pediatric Anxiety Disorders and
Psychopharmacology, Department of
Psychiatry, Duke University Medical Center

"This is an excellent book. It is well written, highly readable, and very informative. A valuable resource, *Treating Anxious Children and Adolescents* contains detailed descriptions of specific techniques and strategies, forms, and other therapeutic material that therapists at all levels of experience will find useful. Rapee, Wignall, Hudson, and Schniering's volume is a welcome addition to the childhood anxiety literature."

—Wendy K. Silverman, Ph.D., Professor
of Psychology at Florida International
University and Director of the Child and
Family Psychosocial Research Center

"*Treating Anxious Children and Adolescents* provides an up-to-date and readable description of both the nature of and the optimal treatment of anxiety in youth. It is both clinically sensitive in its presentation and scientifically respected due to its empirical research support. The work provides an excellent resource for clinicians and researchers working in this important area."

—Philip C. Kendall, Ph.D., ABPP, Professor
and Head, Division of Clinical Psychology,
Temple University

Treating Anxious Children and Adolescents

An Evidence-Based Approach

Ronald M. Rapee, Ph.D., Ann Wignall, M. Psych.,
Jennifer L. Hudson, and Carolyn A. Schniering

NEW HARBINGER PUBLICATIONS, INC.

Publisher's Note

This publication is designed to provide accurate and authoritative information in regard to the subject matter covered. It is sold with the understanding that the publisher is not engaged in rendering psychological, financial, legal, or other professional services. If expert assistance or counseling is needed, the services of a competent professional should be sought.

Distributed in the U.S.A. by Publishers Group West; in Canada by Raincoast Books; in Great Britain by Airlift Book Company, Ltd.; in South Africa by Real Books, Ltd.; in Australia by Boobook; and in New Zealand by Tandem Press.

Copyright © 2000 by Ronald M. Rapee
New Harbinger Publications, Inc.
5674 Shattuck Avenue
Oakland, CA 94609

Cover design © 2000 by Poulson/Gluck
Edited by Donna Long
Text design by Tracy Marie Powell

Library of Congress Catalog Card Number: 99-75287
ISBN 1-57224-192-6 Paperback

Printed in Canada

New Harbinger Publications' Web site address: www.newharbinger.com

02   01   00

10   9   8   7   6   5   4   3   2   1

First printing

To Lucy   —RR

To Michael, Nick, and Tom   —AW

To Angus   —JH

To Simon   —CS

Contents

Acknowledgments

So many people have helped develop our program and our knowledge. In particular, we would like to thank Sian Harris, Kim Begley, and all the interns at the Child and Adolescent Anxiety Clinics at Macquarie University and Royal North Shore hospitals. Thanks also to Paula Barrett and Mark Dadds, who helped develop key parts of the program, and to Phil Kendall, who started it all.

Introduction

Delinquency, sexual abuse, drug abuse . . . there are many serious problems of childhood that tend to grab the major news headlines. Compare those with headlines such as worry, shyness, and nervousness—not quite the same, are they? Traditionally, both the general public and mental health professionals have either ignored anxiety in children or have viewed it as a relatively trivial problem. Public funding, political muscle, and human interest are focused on headline-grabbers and are almost absent for problems such as childhood fears and phobias. Referral rates to child and family mental health units show this bias clearly. The number of referrals of children who are acting out, taking drugs, or are at risk of suicide overwhelms these units. Anxious children are rarely seen. Perhaps it's excusable, in light of this, that many mental health professionals see anxiety in children as a relatively infrequent problem and/or an unremarkable part of a child's development.

Yet, anxiety disorders are the most frequent type of mental disorder in children and adolescents. While the disorders do not usually cause as much disruption as do some other mental disorders, they can result in tremendous personal suffering for children and dramatic interference in their lives. Anxiety in childhood interferes with making friends, with academic achievement and career opportunities, with family cohesion and activities, and with general happiness and self-esteem. In addition, anxious children are much more likely to grow up to be anxious adults—we know that in adulthood, anxiety interferes with work, relationships, and life satisfaction and increases the risk for drug and alcohol abuse, depression, suicide, and medical problems. Anxiety in children therefore needs to be recognized as an important and debilitating problem. Helping kids overcome their anxiety not only improves enjoyment and opportunities for children in the short term, but in the longer term helps prevent the tremendous personal and community costs associated with adult anxiety disorders.

Fortunately, interest in and knowledge of anxiety disorders in children is rapidly expanding. The number of specialist research and treatment clinics directed at anxiety in children has risen dramatically over the past few years worldwide. In addition, the number of individual clinicians and mental health services that are developing an interest and knowledge of the area is growing. Medical practitioners and school counselors are becoming much more knowledgeable in the recognition of these children's problems and in the possibility for treatment. In the past five years, several well-controlled and carefully conducted treatment outcome studies have been published, showing excellent treatment outcome and long-term maintenance results for children with anxiety disorders.

We have been running specialist clinics for anxiety disorders for children between the ages of seven and sixteen for several years. We have seen several hundred children, most of whom have gone on to our treatment program. This program has been based on previous empirically tested programs and has undergone continual modification and updates based on feedback and empirical evaluation. Our success rates have been extremely promising, with over 75 percent of the children experiencing moderate to marked improvements, and these figures have been maintained for at least a year.

About This Book

During the past few years we have regularly been asked to present workshops and training sessions for various groups of mental health professionals with the goal of increasing their knowledge of the nature, assessment, and treatment of anxiety in children. We decided to write this book in order to expand this knowledge base. In addition to covering issues relevant to the nature and assessment of anxiety in children, this book describes a number of techniques and strategies that are important in the treatment of children's anxiety disorders. We have tried to describe these techniques in complete detail to allow even a relatively inexperienced clinician to conduct a successful treatment program. We have organized the book on a technique-by-technique basis rather than session by session, because this method keeps conceptually related material together and allows the clinician flexibility in developing a program suited to their client's particular needs. At the end of this introduction you'll find a comparison of three different treatment programs, but the final program you select will depend on your client and the constraints of your working environment. Each chapter contains suggested forms and exercises to help implement the strategies.

In order to help the therapeutic process, we have also written a handbook for parents: *Helping Your Anxious Child: A Step-by-Step Guide for Parents*. It describes the various strategies in easy-to-follow language for parents of anxious children, and contains forms and suggestions for monitoring and exercises as well. The parent manual is designed to be an adjunct to therapy, not a replacement. The text is meant to emphasize and reinforce your message, and the forms and exercises are the same as the ones covered in this book. We have found that using a parent manual of this type increases the learning that clients engage in and allows the therapist more time and opportunity to focus on the individualized aspects of therapy such as tailoring the program to suit the particular client and ensuring the motivation and engagement of the client.

Before beginning the main section of the book, there are a few practical issues to discuss.

Terminology and Age Effects

Naturally, children at different ages and stages of development can have quite different needs and responses. Therefore, wherever possible we will try to suggest variations to the strategies according to the age group of the child. The words used to describe these different age groups can vary between professionals and can become quite confusing, so we have decided to use the terms "child" or "children" generically to refer to the full range of children and adolescents. When needed, we will use the term "younger child" to refer to children below twelve years of age, and the term "adolescent" to refer to adolescents older than twelve.

In general, our discussions will be relevant to children between the ages of roughly seven to sixteen because those are the ages we have had the most direct experience with. For children under the age of seven, we assume that very similar techniques are appropriate, although with lower age greater parental involvement would be required. For example, we have run a very successful program for anxious four-year-old children that covered procedures very similar to the ones in this book, but in which only the parents attended treatment sessions. We are now running a large-scale controlled trial of this program.

We would conceptualize and treat the older adolescent (someone older than sixteen) largely as an adult; the standard treatments for anxiety in adults would be applicable with appropriate concessions for age.

Group versus Individual Treatment

Another relevant issue is whether the treatment should be run in a group or individual format. The simple answer is: either one. Our early research at the University of Queensland involved individual treatment, and results were excellent (Barrett, Dadds, and Rapee 1996). In our more recent programs we have conducted primarily group treatment and results have been at least as good (Rapee 1996). Whether you choose to run your program in a group or individual format is up to you and will no doubt be based largely on practical considerations.

In this book, most chapters are from the perspective of treatment with an individual family, but in most cases the application to a group format will not be very different. Where there are clearly different issues or different methods of delivery, we have tried to address those as much as possible within the relevant sections. Finally, we have included an appendix that gives a more detailed discussion of considerations regarding group application.

Diagnostic Differences

Writing a book in which all anxious children are considered together raises the issue of diagnostic differences. The way we conceptualize things, the similarities between the various anxiety disorders far outweigh any differences, especially with respect to treatment considerations. For this reason, throughout this book we write about treatment of anxiety in children in a fairly generic way. The vast majority of treatment procedures will be common across all of the anxiety disorders. Where there are relevant differences in specific application, we will discuss them.

Similarly, when we have run group treatment at our clinic, we do not separate the groups according to different anxiety disorders. This has worked well for us so far. The children do not seem to let the minor differences isolate them and they pick up on the marked similarities. In addition, grouping children who are anxious about slightly different things allows them to help each other.

Including the Family

When conducting treatment with children, a decision always needs to be made as to the degree of involvement of other members of the family. In an early treatment-outcome study (Barrett et al. 1996), we demonstrated that treatment of anxious children was considerably better when the parents of the children were included than when the children were treated alone. Interestingly, however, this difference was very marked for children under the age of eleven but was not really apparent for those eleven and older. Nevertheless, clinically there seem to be benefits in including parents in treatment, even for adolescents. We suggest including parents in treatment for all anxious children, but this is especially important for younger children.

Including other family members is a good idea if those people play a major role in caregiving. Our general conception of the inclusion of parents in treatment is that parents act, in a sense, as twenty-four-hour per day therapists. In other words, though the conceptual focus of treatment is the anxious child, the parents are included both to learn the techniques that the child learns (so that they can help with application) and also to learn how they themselves can change their behavior to help the child. For this reason, anyone who plays a major role in caregiving could be included in the sessions. In addition, anyone who appears to be contributing to the child's anxiety should also be included. As with any treatment for children, consistency is important. If the child is spending time with more than one person, all should become informed of the treatment procedures. This does not necessarily mean that they all have to be physically present at the sessions—who comes to sessions will be a matter of practicalities. Ideally, however, all caregivers, no matter how minor, need to be informed of what the program is teaching the child and what the goals of treatment are. In intact families, we strongly encourage both parents to attend sessions if possible. There is little point in having one parent help with all the strategies if the other parent is unknowingly undermining them. In cases where parents are separated but the child continues to spend independent time with both, we also encourage both parents to attend as long as any hostility between them can be kept under control. There is little point in having both parents attend sessions if the sessions simply turn into arguments. When a stepparent is in the family and plays an influential role in parenting, we encourage that person to attend sessions. We once treated a child who was accompanied by two separated parents and their respective new partners. Of course, this is usually not a recommended practice due to the potential for sessions taking on an alternative agenda.

In some cases, siblings may also be invited to attend some sessions. As we will discuss later, it can sometimes be very valuable to use siblings to help model or role-play certain strategies. However, we would not usually include other children from the family in the overall treatment program unless those children were also anxious and were therefore the focus of the same treatment. Including nonanxious children is likely to alter the focus of treatment and disrupt the overall process. Including extended family members who are not directly involved in caregiving is also likely to disrupt the sessions due to the sheer size of the unit and the various personal agendas that might have to be dealt with.

As discussed later in this book, when we run the actual sessions we typically have certain periods in each session that are devoted to the child alone, some to the parents alone, and some to the family as a group. In our most common scenario, we begin each session by seeing the parents and child together. We then move on to time alone with either the child or the parents, followed by time with the other party. We finish the session by summarizing the goals of the session and assigning homework for the parents and child.

Some Sample Programs

As we mentioned earlier, we have written this book in a technique-focused manner to allow greater flexibility in application. Our current program is conducted in nine sessions over an eleven-week period. However, other programs have extended to as many as sixteen sessions. In the table below, we show the schedule for our current nine-session program as well as a suggested briefer program for managed-care purposes and a longer program for more complicated treatments. These suggested programs are in addition to a prior thorough assessment and should be interpreted flexibly, especially in the case of individual treatment. It should be noted that, as yet, we have not tested the efficacy of the managed-care program, although we have shown good effects in a one-week intensive program for rural children and a six-session parent-education program for four-year-old children.

The key strategy in our view is exposure. Exposure needs to be introduced as early as possible and given plenty of time and practice. Prior to beginning exposure, cognitive restructuring is useful for setting the scene for exposure and helping to make it more effective. When there is time, relaxation techniques can also provide a valuable coping strategy that can help smooth the way for exposure. For specific cases, especially children with broader and more complex problems, the later addition of assertiveness training and social skills as well as discussion of bullying and teasing can be a valuable adjunct to treatment.

Table 1: Sample Treatment Programs

Session	Our Current Program	Managed Care Program	Extended Program
1	Rapport building; linking thoughts and feelings; nature of anxiety.	Rapport building; linking thoughts and feelings; nature of anxiety. Introduction to cognitive restructuring.	Rapport building; linking thoughts and feelings; nature of anxiety.
2	Introduction to cognitive restructuring.	Cognitive restructuring practice; child management.	Introduction to cognitive restructuring.
3	Cognitive restructuring practice; self-rewards; child management.	Commencement of graded exposure.	Cognitive restructuring practice; self-rewards; child management.
4	Commencement of graded exposure.	Review use of techniques.	Introduction to relaxation. Practice of techniques.
5	Review use of techniques.	Review use of techniques.*	Practice of relaxation and cognitive restructuring.
6	Review use of techniques; introduce social-skills practice.	Review use of techniques; termination issues; closure.	Commencement of graded exposure.
7	Review use of techniques; discuss assertiveness and teasing.*		Review use of techniques.
8	Review use of techniques.*		Review use of techniques; introduce social-skills practice.

9	Termination issues; closure.		Review use of techniques; discuss assertiveness and teasing.*
10			Review use of techniques.*
11			Review use of techniques.*
12			Termination issues; closure.

Note: Sessions marked with an asterisk should be followed by at least a two-week break to allow time for practice.

Chapter 1

Assessment and Diagnosis of Anxiety Disorders

The symptoms of anxiety disorders in children are very similar to those found in adults. According to the *Diagnostic and Statistical Manual of Mental Disorders*, or *DSM-IV*, the following common diagnoses can be made in children: separation anxiety disorder, generalized anxiety disorder, social phobia, specific phobia, obsessive-compulsive disorder, panic disorder with or without agoraphobia, post-traumatic stress disorder, acute stress disorder, and adjustment disorder. Of these, the diagnoses that are found most frequently are separation anxiety disorder, generalized anxiety disorder, and social phobia. Later in this chapter, we also identify another problem that is not listed in the *DSM-IV*—school phobia.

The various subtypes of anxiety share many similar features, and differ primarily in the specific focus of the fear. Children experience anxiety in response to a perceived threat in their environment, and while the types of stimuli perceived as threatening vary from one anxiety disorder to the next, the anxiety response tends to be similar. When they are anxious, these children focus excessively on the negative outcomes that may occur, experience many somatic changes, and go to great lengths to avoid threatening situations. It should be noted that some authors have viewed obsessive compulsive disorder as somewhat different to the other anxiety disorders (March and Male 1998).

Common Diagnoses

Separation Anxiety Disorder

Children with separation anxiety disorder have excessive anxiety about separation from caregivers to whom they are emotionally attached. They worry that some harm or tragedy will occur to those they love, leading to loss or long-term separation. For example, one young boy with separation anxiety disorder believed that if his mother went out to see a movie with his father, she would be killed, either in the car while traveling there or while watching the movie. Separation fears are most commonly centered on the primary caregiver—usually the mother—but fathers, grandparents, and other family members can sometimes be included.

Children with separation anxiety experience a great deal of distress on separation or even the threat of separation. They cry, plead desperately with the caregiver, and may throw tantrums. They are often clingy, and like to stay in close proximity to the caregiver. Somatic complaints such as headaches, nausea, and vomiting are common. They may experience nightmares involving themes of separation, death, and loss, and may have associated sleep difficulties. They do whatever is within their power to avoid separating from important attachment figures: they avoid situations such as attending school, sleeping alone, playing at other friends' homes, and staying away overnight. The disorder is most typical of younger children and is less common in adolescents. When making the diagnosis of separation anxiety, it is important to ensure that the anxiety is inappropriate to the child's developmental level and is not within the normal range of behaviors for their age.

Generalized Anxiety Disorder

Children and adolescents with generalized anxiety disorder are commonly described as "worriers" by their parents. They worry excessively about many areas of life functioning, such as schoolwork, family, friends, health, and any new or unusual situation. As a general guideline for making this diagnosis, the worry needs to be more days than not for a minimum of six months. These children show a persistent tendency to make negative predictions and to presume that the worst possible outcome will occur. For example, one twelve-year-old girl was certain that she would perform poorly in a school examination and that this would then mean she would never be able to pursue a successful career. This belief lead to chronic worry and high anxiety about schoolwork, poor concentration and attention, and, in turn, to reduced academic performance.

Children with generalized anxiety disorder report difficulties controlling the worry and often seek reassurance or comfort from others. Over time, constant reassurance can further reinforce negative beliefs. Despite a common belief that generalized anxiety disorder is manifested only as worry, these children will show considerable avoidance behavior—for example, refusing to try anything new or unusual. Other associated problems include poor concentration, irritability, restlessness, fatigue, sleep disturbance, and somatic symptoms such as muscle tension, headaches, or stomachaches.

Social Phobia

Children with social phobia are highly fearful of social or performance situations in which they are exposed to unfamiliar people or possible evaluation. They fear that they will do something or act in a way that will result in humiliation or embarrassment. In brief, they fear that others will negatively evaluate them. For example, one sixteen-year-old boy was very anxious about asking a girl at school out on a date. He worried that he would make mistakes and stutter while asking her out. He thought that she would reject him and think he was a fool, resulting in total humiliation. Older children and adolescents are typically able to recognize that their fears are excessive or unrealistic. This is not always the case with younger children, who may lack insight into the extreme nature of their fears.

When faced with social or performance situations, socially phobic children experience intense anxiety and distress. Younger children will cry, freeze, withdraw, or hide behind people to whom they are emotionally attached. The anxiety in social situations is associated with physiological changes such as nausea, stomachaches, blushing, sweating, trembling, heart palpitations, and dizziness. Young people with social phobia are so fearful of negative evaluation that they avoid social or performance situations in any way they can. Commonly avoided situations include public speaking, meeting new people, eating in public, playing sports, attending parties, speaking in class, and speaking to authority figures. When avoidance is not possible, the situations are endured with intense anxiety. The distress and avoidance of social situations interferes markedly with daily functioning, and in some children may hinder social-emotional development. Children and adolescents with severe social phobia tend to have few friends, be involved in few recreational or extracurricular activities, and may have poor social skills.

Specific Phobia

Children with specific phobias have excessive fears of particular objects or situations such as the dark, animals, heights, or blood. When confronted with the specific stimulus, the children become anxious and distressed. As with the other anxiety disorders, children with specific phobias will avoid the feared object or situation whenever they can, or endure it with anxiety. These patterns of fear and avoidance can interfere with the young person's normal routine. In making a diagnosis, however, it is important to remember that mild fears during childhood are fairly common and should not be confused with phobias. Fears are considered to be specific phobias only if the degree of anxiety and avoidance is clearly excessive compared to other children their age, and interferes markedly with areas of life functioning.

Obsessive-Compulsive Disorder

Children with obsessive-compulsive disorder experience persistent obsessions and compulsions. Obsessions are recurrent thoughts, images, or urges that are intrusive and distressing. Compulsions are repetitive behaviors that are performed in response to obsessions, and are aimed at preventing negative events. Common types of intrusive thoughts reported by young people include concerns about harming others or themselves, contamination, superstitious ideas about bad luck or karma, and religious concerns. Common compulsions include washing or cleaning, checking, repeating rituals, ordering, and hoarding or saving. Compulsions sometimes involve other people, such as family members. For example, a child may require a specific verbal response in order to complete a ritual.

Children with obsessive-compulsive disorder perform compulsions following an obsession in order to prevent a feared outcome from occurring. After the compulsion has been carried out, they usually experience an immediate decrease in their level of distress. However, this decrease is typically short lived, because doubt or other triggers in the environment can result in further intrusive thoughts. It is not uncommon for children or adolescents to feel the need to perform a ritual five times or more. As a general guideline for making this diagnosis, the compulsions must last more than an hour per day. Typically the obsessions and constant compulsions become highly frustrating and time-consuming for the individual. Avoidance of cues in the environment that trigger intrusive thoughts are common. This often leads to marked life interference and feelings of depression.

For example, one fifteen-year-old girl experienced intrusive thoughts every time she used the toilet. Her intrusive thought was, "If I don't wash my hands thoroughly with soap, I will infect the rest of my family with germs, and they will get very sick." In response to this thought, she would meticulously wash her hands with soap for around five minutes after she used the toilet. As she walked away from the bathroom, she would experience further intrusive thoughts, such as, "I haven't gotten rid of all the germs yet and could still infect people." She would then perform more hand washing. This cycle would typically continue for long periods until she felt satisfied that there were no longer any germs on her hands, and her anxiety level would then drop. Over time, her hands became chaffed and sore from the constant washing, further increasing her distress.

While adolescents can generally recognize the unrealistic nature of their thoughts and behaviors, younger children can lack insight. Younger children may be reluctant, or unable, to verbalize the nature of their obsessions due to a limited understanding of their difficulties, language limitations, or embarrassment. In such cases parent reports and behavioral observation of compulsions are a necessary source of information.

Panic Disorder with or without Agoraphobia

Children with panic disorder experience recurrent, unexpected episodes of intense anxiety known as panic attacks. Panic attacks involve short bursts of severe fear or discomfort, during which several bodily symptoms, such as sweating, trembling, shortness of breath, dizziness, and heart palpitations are experienced. Children who panic become frightened of their bodily changes, as do adults with the disorder. They typically misinterpret their physical symptoms as an indication that something is wrong or that they are losing control. As the child becomes older, he or she might begin to connect symptoms with thoughts of going crazy or dying. When they experience an attack, they typically feel the need to escape from their present surroundings, such as the classroom. They worry about having further attacks, and may start to avoid situations where it would be difficult for them to escape or to get help in the case of an attack. If avoidance is more than minimal, a diagnosis of panic disorder with agoraphobia would be warranted. Situations that children commonly avoid include crowded environments, public transport, movie theaters, school classrooms, and generally leaving home.

In our experience, panic disorder is not common until late adolescence, and is very rare before puberty. It appears that panic disorder is often incorrectly diagnosed in children. While it is not uncommon for children to report that they felt "panicky" in specific situations, this would not necessarily constitute a panic attack. Similarly, panic attacks can be seen in the context of other disorders, in which case a separate diagnosis of panic disorder may not be warranted. This issue is discussed in greater detail later in this chapter.

Post-Traumatic Stress Disorder and Related Conditions

Children with post-traumatic stress disorder display a set of characteristic symptoms that develop following exposure to a traumatic, physically threatening event. Children show many of the same features of post-traumatic stress disorder that adults do, although in children the specific expression of each symptom may be slightly different. They re-experience the trauma in various ways, such as via distressing recollections, dreams of the event, or distress at exposure to cues that remind them of the event. Children with post-traumatic stress disorder avoid such cues, and generally show increased arousal when exposed to or reminded of the trauma-related cues. Younger children may report more generalized dreams of monsters, of rescuing others, or of threats to self or others. Themes related to the trauma often emerge during play. For example, younger children may repeatedly enact killings with human figures or animals, create places of danger for toys, or enact crashes with vehicles. Younger children with post-traumatic stress disorder may be unable to verbalize the nature of their fears or the extent of their distress. In such cases, behavioral observation and parental report provide important assessment information.

A related disorder, acute stress disorder, has only been introduced with the publication of the *DSM-IV*. The features are very similar to those of post-traumatic stress disorder, but the diagnosis can be made within the first month following trauma (post-traumatic stress disorder requires at least one month of persistent disturbance). Where a child appears to be distressed by a stressful life event but does not meet the full criteria for acute stress disorder or post-traumatic stress disorder, he or she may be more likely to meet criteria for an adjustment disorder, which refers to a clearly defined stressor in a child's life.

School Phobia

School phobia, or school refusal, does not appear in the *DSM-IV* as a separate diagnostic category. This problem refers to a set of behaviors that are associated with other anxiety diagnoses, most commonly with separation anxiety disorder or social phobia. Children with school refusal experience varying degrees of symptom severity and life interference. The features of school refusal include complaints of school and reluctance to attend, progressing to total refusal to go to school or to remain there. These children experience severe distress at the time of departure for school, including a range of somatic complaints such as nausea, headaches, and dizziness. Behavioral reactions such as tears, fits of temper, and even aggressive outbursts are also common, particularly when the child is forced to attend school. The excessive somatic complaints associated with school refusal may be interpreted by parents as a medical problem, resulting in visits to the doctor and more time away from school.

Several unique features of school refusal merit discussion. In some cases school refusal may be closely linked with dysfunctional patterns of behavior within the family. Parents who have some form of emotional disturbance may be difficult to work with as they may be receiving certain benefits from having their child at home with them. In this case, the problem may lie primarily with the parent rather than the child. Alternately, school refusal may be a sign of oppositionality and poor behavior management, more so than anxiety and fear.

School-refusal behavior can be motivated by a range of factors, including fear of separation, fear of negative evaluation, dysfunctional family dynamics, and behavior-management problems. During the assessment phase it is important to identify the factors that are crucial in the maintenance of the school-refusal behavior. School refusal motivated by anxiety can be treated using the same techniques outlined for the other anxiety disorders, but targeted specifically for the school situation. However, if family features also appear to be maintaining the problem, additional treatment addressing family issues and/or behavior management will be necessary. This will mean working more extensively with the family and seeking individual treatment for parents where appropriate.

Diagnostic and Assessment Issues

Assessment of Normal versus Clinical Anxiety

During their development, children experience normal fears and anxiety that undergo natural changes from infancy through to adolescence. Normal fears during infancy include fears of loud noises, strangers, and separation. During the school years, fears of evaluative and social situations, bodily injury, and illness become more salient. Similarly, the content of chronic worry in children follows a progression from physical threats to less concrete threats. Apparently, children become more capable of generating severe generalized anxiety, through worry, as their cognitive abilities develop. General worry about various areas of functioning, and performance anxiety and shyness in situations that involve unfamiliar people, are common in both children and adults.

Normal fear and anxiety in children differs from clinically significant anxiety primarily in severity, not in quality. In considering whether anxiety is clinically significant, our guiding principle is determining whether it causes the child marked distress or impairment in important areas of life such as school, social relationships, or family functioning. To begin with, it is important to obtain specific, behavioral descriptions of how the anxiety is interfering in the child's life. You need to know how many areas of the child's life are affected, and the nature and extent of the interference in each area. You need to know whether the anxiety is a problem on a daily basis, or every few weeks or months. If the anxiety interferes with daily life, approximately how many hours are affected each day? When distinguishing "normal" from clinical anxiety, it is useful to determine whether or not the child's behavior and distress are clearly excessive compared with other children their age. The duration and pervasiveness of the difficulties, and the extent to which they can be controlled, are further distinguishing features between clinical and nonclinical anxiety. For example, it is not unusual for children and adolescents to experience worry and anxiety, but the worry associated with generalized anxiety disorder is difficult to control, pervasive, and chronic.

In addition, a clear indication of the level of distress experienced by the child is needed. There is a vast difference between a child who is mildly bothered by a situation and a child who totally freezes up with fear. Highly specific information is needed regarding the extent to which the child is upset by his anxiety. It is important to gain an understanding of the types of situations in which the child becomes upset, how often and how long he is upset, and the level of distress that is experienced. Finding out if the *child* is distressed about his anxiety (or whether only the parents or other family members are distressed) is critical. We have seen families in which the child was not overly concerned about his difficulties, though the parents were distressed about the child. In such cases, perhaps the problem lies more with the parents' views of the child rather than within the child himself. Of course, some children may not be willing to report their distress, which needs to be taken into account.

Differential Diagnosis

Children and adolescents with a wide range of difficulties can be difficult to diagnose. Highly detailed and specific information about the nature, duration, and severity of symptoms is essential when differentiating between diagnoses. In most cases, the anxiety disorders can be differentiated from each other by examining the central focus of the fears. For example, we have found that it is common for adolescents to report panic-like symptoms in threatening situations. Children with separation or social fears are particularly likely to report feeling "panicky" in situations involving separation or possible scrutiny by others. However, in most cases a diagnosis of panic disorder would not be warranted for several reasons. To begin with, the symptoms are often not severe enough to constitute a true panic attack. Similarly, even where symptomatic criteria are met for a panic attack, the attacks are usually not unexpected, and are limited to specific situations. However, most importantly, the central fear is commonly related to something other than the somatic changes associated with a panic attack. The central distinction between panic attacks in panic disorder and attacks in the context of other anxiety disorders is that the primary fear in panic disorder is of the bodily changes, rather than of other types of threat such as negative evaluation or separation. Where panic attacks occur only in the context of another childhood anxiety disorder, a separate diagnosis of panic disorder is not warranted. Therefore, in order to make an accurate diagnosis, it is crucial to gain an understanding of both the specific symptoms experienced when the client feels panicky and the negative thoughts behind the panic.

Similarly, fear of embarrassment or humiliation to some degree may be present in children with generalized anxiety, separation anxiety, or specific phobias, but a separate diagnosis of social phobia may not be warranted if this fear is not the main issue for the child. For example, a child with separation anxiety disorder may cry when he goes to school based on a fear that his mother will be killed while he is there. He may also become embarrassed about crying in front of other children. However, given that the embarrassment is not the main focus of the fear in this situation, a diagnosis of social phobia would not be warranted. Again, detailed investigation into the central focus of the anxiety is needed to distinguish social phobia from the other anxiety disorders.

The excessive worry of generalized anxiety can be distinguished from the types of worries seen in other anxiety disorders in children. To begin with, the worry in generalized anxiety is different from the obsessional thoughts seen in obsessive-compulsive disorder. Obsessional thoughts are usually not restricted to excessive worries about real-life problems, but tend to involve more bizarre intrusions that can come as urges and images as well as thoughts. Children with generalized anxiety disorder worry about many different real-life problems rather than about one theme—such as separation or negative evaluation—as is the case with separation anxiety disorder and social phobia. Excessive worries about everyday situations are also common in mood and psychotic disorders, but a separate diagnosis of generalized anxiety disorder should not be given if the worry occurs exclusively during the course of these other difficulties.

Finally, differentiating between the anxiety disorders and other childhood disorders can be difficult. We have found that marked avoidance of situations may be interpreted as disobedience by teachers or significant others. The disobedience seen in the externalizing disorders is generally motivated by the payoffs in a situation. This is very distinct from the noncompliance sometimes seen in anxious children, which is motivated by avoidance of the negatives in the situation. In other words, an anxious child will avoid because of the risk of danger in a situation (such as humiliation or injury), whereas an oppositional child will avoid because of the positives he may get from this behavior (playing computer games at home all day). In some cases both motivations may be at work simultaneously and each may have to be addressed in therapy.

Severe avoidance and withdrawal may also be interpreted as depression. Again, it is important to determine whether behaviors are related to avoidance of possible threat or whether they are driven by a lack of motivation and pleasure from activities. Children who are psychotic or who have pervasive developmental disorders such as Asberger's syndrome may also show withdrawal, particularly in social situations. With these disorders, avoidance or withdrawal is driven by a lack of interest in relating to others. This is quite different from children with social phobia, who tend to be interested in social contact with familiar people but avoid strangers because of the potential for negative evaluation. In each of the above cases, the function of the behaviors is the key differentiating feature between the childhood disorders. Where children experience a wide range of problems, making an accurate diagnosis requires as thorough an understanding as possible of the specific focus of the fears and the motivation behind the behaviors. Ultimately, distinguishing anxiety disorders from other childhood difficulties is more important for effective treatment than differentiating between anxiety disorders.

Comorbidity

Children with anxiety disorders are very likely to have a concurrent diagnosis of an additional anxiety disorder or another childhood disorder (this is discussed in more detail in the next chapter). Children with a high degree of symptom overlap across various diagnostic categories can be difficult to assess; discrete diagnoses may be unclear when many symptoms are present at the same time. Good skills at differential diagnosis are needed to tease apart various disorders. As previously discussed, obtaining very specific, behavioral details about the nature of the presenting problems is critical. This should include information about the severity, duration, frequency, and core cognitive features of the various problems. It is also useful to look at the onset of the difficulties, in order to gain a sense of the development of symptoms over time. Be familiar with the characteristic features of the various childhood disorders, and ask direct questions pertaining to these features.

Once the presence of concurrent diagnoses has been established, the next step is to determine which is the principal diagnosis and which are the additional diagnoses. Traditionally in psychiatry, the primary diagnosis is defined as the disorder that developed first over the course of time. *We* use the term "principal diagnosis" to refer to the disorder that is most problematic in the child's life. Indicators of the extent to which the problems are interfering or distressing for the child are therefore needed to distinguish the principal diagnosis from any additional diagnoses. Again, very detailed information is needed about the way in which the problems interfere with various areas of functioning and the ways in which they cause the child distress. We have found it useful to directly ask each family member what they see as the biggest problem and why. Similarly, you can ask the family which of the problems they would most like help with or which is most disruptive in their lives. Ask them which problem they would remove if they had magical powers that could instantly take away only one problem. Ultimately, your own impression as a therapist should guide you in deciding the principal and additional diagnoses.

Once you have identified all of the existing disorders and the degree to which they each interfere with the child's life, it will be necessary to determine if an anxiety disorder is the most logical first point of intervention. Certain conditions will require urgent addressing ahead of anxiety, such as drug and alcohol dependence, suicidal ideation, or severe weight loss. In addition, the existence of some of these conditions may interfere with treatment of other problems and will therefore demand attention first. For example, the adolescent who is abusing drugs will not be able to attend clearly to anxiety-reduction strategies until the acute drug abuse has stopped, even if the anxiety disorder is the more dominant and possibly underlying problem.

In dealing with comorbid conditions, the main strategy is to approach the problems systematically. One cannot simply attack a new issue each week or the client will never be able to follow the techniques. There are many similarities in the treatment strategies for each disorder and these can be integrated into a program that aims first to address the principal disorder but addresses additional disorders in a parallel fashion. For example, in dealing with a child who meets criteria for a principal diagnosis of separation anxiety disorder and an additional diagnosis of oppositional defiant disorder, a central component of treatment will include child-management strategies. Treatment for the separation anxiety will include teaching the parent strategies to help manage the child differently, including reducing any overinvolvement and increasing consistency (this is discussed in more detail in chapter 7). As the principal disorder, this would be the first focus. However, child-management strategies such as consistency are also a central component of treatments for oppositional disorder. Therefore, once the parent has mastered the general strategies for child management and has learned to apply them to the separation fears, therapy could focus on applying similar strategies to the oppositional behavior. In fact, application of the strategies to some of the low-level oppositional behaviors could be used to illustrate and practice the value of the strategies for separation fears. Thus, treatment of the additional disorder does not need to wait until treatment of the principal disorder is complete—treatments can be integrated in a parallel fashion. The key is to remain clear and systematic, and to clearly indicate your aims and strategies to the client.

Another issue is addressing treatment toward the underlying motivations. Treatment of superficial behaviors is considerably less important than is modification of the motivations and attitudes underlying them. As we mentioned earlier, two disorders may share common behaviors, but the behaviors may be motivated by differing purposes. Consider the child in the preceding example who has both separation anxiety disorder and oppositional defiant disorder. This child may refuse to go to school due to a fear of leaving Mom, but may soon learn that not going to school is fun. Both the fear of separation and the rewards of staying home and having fun may motivate school nonattendance. It is essential that you consider all the possible motivations for a given behavior and regularly reassess the child and modify your hypotheses. This case illustrates the principle that, despite the development of manual-based therapies, there is no substitute for a clear formulation for each case. In the case of this child, simply implementing exposure to the fear of separation would not return him to school. Exposure would need to be combined with a change in the rewards obtained by staying home and not going to school.

Empirically, we have failed to find marked differences in the response to our programs between children with and without comorbid diagnoses. The existence of oppositional problems, attention deficit disorder, depression, and even mild intellectual disorder do not seem to affect treatment outcome in an obvious way. However, a clear formulation and an integrative program that systematically addresses all problems is important.

Building Rapport and Credibility

At the beginning of the session you'll want to build some credibility, both for yourself and the program. Introduce yourself and your experience with these types of problems, briefly describe some of the outcome data from studies on the treatment of child anxiety, and describe your own success with these problems.

Much of your early work should be conducted with the family as a whole, especially for younger children. However, it is a good idea to repeat some of the information gathering and rapport building with the child and the parents separately, when it comes time to see each alone. With adolescents it is particularly important to spend more time building rapport with them on their own and letting them feel that you respect their independence and individuality. Structure the interview so that at some point you see the young person alone—this is critical because it allows them to express concerns about safety or other issues in the absence of their caregivers.

We did not intend for this book to provide general counseling and therapy skills; we assume that you already have a good knowledge and experience of generic psychotherapeutic skills. Naturally, all of your usual microskills and interpersonal abilities need to be used for anxious families as for any others. However, we will briefly mention a couple of points that are especially relevant to families of anxious children.

Anxiety runs in families, so you are likely to find, at the initial stages, high degrees of anxiety in the entire family. Of course, the target child will be feeling anxious. She is likely to be worried about what is expected of her, what you may be thinking of her, and what you will be forcing her to do. In addition, the parents or caregivers may be generally nervous as to what you think of them as caregivers, whether you are looking into their own personalities, and what they are going to have to do. You can help rapport by preempting some of these concerns and allaying them. You may want to ask the family if they have any concerns, what they think therapy is all about, and what they think you think of them. However, depending on the degree of such things as suspicion or social anxiety, they may not yet be ready to answer these questions openly. Instead, be prepared to anticipate such concerns. Let the family know up front that you are making no judgments about them and that they will be in control at all times: it is up to them what they talk about and how much they do. You may also want to remind them of the confidentiality of what is said in sessions. Simply through your manner, questions, and comments, you can impart a sense that you are listening to your clients and that they are not being judged. Most anxious families are very easy to engage and will relax very quickly after the opening stages.

In some cases, the child may be extremely anxious and refuse to answer, or may answer only in monosyllables. Frequently, anxious children fake being "good"—that is, they try to provide answers that they think you want or that cast them in a good light. In these cases, you may want to reduce the pressure on the child early on and conduct more of the rapport building and information gathering with the parents (perhaps while the child is present in the room). In such cases it will be even more important to spend time alone with the child and work on building rapport. Sometimes, especially with younger children, there may be little progress on this front in the first week or so. Remove the focus from "problems" all together and simply try to engage the child in conversation. Hobbies, movies, and books can all be good topics as long as you don't look as though you are trying too hard to be a friend. Sometimes, playing a game is a good way to break the ice, especially with younger children. (We have had good success with Pictionary.) Anxious children will also need plenty of positive feedback and encouragement for their efforts in engaging with you. Appropriate feedback should help them feel more comfortable and hence more able to talk about their difficulties. Positive reinforcement in the form of stickers or stamps can work in some cases with younger children.

Ask the child what she knows about why she has come to see you. Children often have fears related to the assessment—that they will get into trouble, be taken away from their parents, or that they are going crazy. Unfortunately, anxious children are often told very little about the assessment, so you can help the child relax by outlining the purpose and structure of the assessment and the type of treatment that you will be conducting. They need to be made aware that they will not be in trouble and that they will not be forced to do anything they don't want to. They should also be reassured that lots of children come to see you and they are not going crazy.

The Diagnostic Interview

The purpose of the diagnostic interview is to gather sufficient information to come to a basic conceptualization of the presenting problems, incorporating both psychological and behavioral factors that may be involved in the maintenance of the difficulties. This conceptualization should then guide diagnosis and treatment.

Having established rapport, the next step is to focus on understanding the presenting complaints and gathering relevant background information. Current thinking on child assessment emphasizes the importance of obtaining information from children, in addition to information from other significant people in the child's life. Children have been shown to provide a unique insight to their own anxieties, although this needs to be weighed against the fact that sometimes young children may not be good at reporting on their internal states. Important details include the severity and frequency of behaviors, and patterns of reinforcement relating to the behaviors in the family. The extent to which the child is seeking and receiving reassurance should be looked at in detail. A developmental and medical history should be obtained, including details about the birth, developmental milestones, the attachments formed during the early years, and the commencement of school. A full school history should be recorded, including progress, any specific learning difficulties, interactions with peers, performance on examinations, attendance record, and homework habits. General information about anxiety and other problems in the family history should be obtained. Finally, parents' views and current management of the child's anxiety are important for a thorough formulation.

Structured Diagnostic Interviews

Structured or semistructured interviews have several advantages over unstructured interviews. Unstructured interviews generally have poor reliability and lack objectivity. Structured interviews provide data that are easily quantifiable and that assist in making a formal diagnosis. Several structured interviews have been developed specifically for children, including the Diagnostic Interview Schedule for Children (DISC-R; Shaffer et al. 1993), the Kiddie SADS—Present and Lifetime Version (K-SADS-PL; Kaufman et al. 1996), and the Anxiety Disorders Interview Schedule for *DSM-IV*: Child Version (ADIS-IV-C; Silverman and Albano 1996). These interviews are now widely used in research and some clinical settings. They contain both parent and child components, are suitable for children between six and seventeen years, and take between one and two hours to complete. Most of these diagnostic interviews have undergone revision in the last decade, in order to parallel changes in diagnostic classification systems or to improve reliability. The DISC-R and the K-SADS-PL are each designed to screen for a wide range of childhood disorders and have a subset of questions devoted to the screening of anxiety. These items cover most of the subcategories of anxiety seen in children and adolescents. By contrast, the ADIS-IV-C focuses mainly on the assessment of anxiety in children and adolescents, though it does also screen briefly for the other childhood disorders. It contains specific items that address the nature and severity of anxiety as well as the extent of avoidance, precipitating events, cognitive cues, and distress and life interference.

Interrater agreement on the outcome of structured interviews with anxious children is generally moderate to high (Rapee et al. 1994). This suggests that anxiety disorders can be reliably diagnosed in children and adolescents using structured interviews. However, the test-retest reliability of children's reports over time, and the extent of agreement between parent and child reports, are potential points of concern. The test-retest reliability of diagnoses of anxiety disorders based on children's self-reports are adequate, but the consistency of self-reports of individual symptoms over time is questionable (Schniering, Hudson, and Rapee in press). In addition, one commonly finds moderate to poor agreement between parent and child reports (Rapee et al. 1994). Children tend to report fewer symptoms than do parents, and they tend to be unreliable in reporting complex details such as the duration and frequency of anxiety-related symptoms. There are several possible explanations for low parent-child agreement in the assessment of child anxiety. As previously noted, parents may have difficulty understanding the exact features of their child's difficulties, or may read their own anxiety into their child's behaviors. Or the discrepancy may be due to other factors related to the child, such as difficulty understanding the items or social desirability (Schniering, Hudson, and Rapee in press). Alternately, perhaps widely varying reports reflect different but equally valid perceptions of the problem (Kazdin, French, and Unis 1983). The limited research into the validity of diagnostic interviews suggests that they provide fairly accurate information on the primary features of anxiety in children and adolescents and are able to discriminate between various diagnostic groups reasonably well (Schniering, Hudson, and Rapee in press).

Self-Report Measures

There are several self-report measures designed specifically to assess anxiety in children and adolescents (see table 2). These questionnaires are quick and easy to administer, and provide information on the nature and severity of anxiety-related symptoms. They are designed to be used as an adjunct to a thorough clinical interview, and should not be used as the basis of a diagnosis. Normative data are available for each of these measures and are useful for assessing severity and treatment outcome. Research has shown that these measures have adequate test-retest reliability and validity (Schniering, Hudson, and Rapee in press). In other words, the questionnaires produce approximately the same information each time they are administered and they are reasonably accurate measures of anxiety-related symptoms in children.

Table 2: Self-Report Measures of Anxiety in Children

Measure	Reference
Revised Children's Manifest Anxiety Scale (RCMAS)	Reynolds and Richmond 1978
State-Trait Anxiety Inventory for Children (STAIC)	Spielberger 1973
Fear Survey Schedule for Children Revised (FSSC-R)	Ollendick 1983
Social Phobia and Anxiety Inventory for Children (SPAI-C)	Beidel, Turner, and Morris 1995
Spence Children's Anxiety Scale (SCAS)	Spence 1997
Multidimensional Anxiety Scale for Children (MASC)	March 1998
Screen for Child Anxiety Related Emotional Disorders (SCARED)	Birmaher et al. 1997

The measures were developed to target different aspects of anxiety in children. Key features of each of the measures, including the primary focus, the subscales, the item structure, and the age range for which they are suitable, are presented in table 3. Clearly, structure and content vary considerably across measures. The scale you choose will depend on factors such as the age of the child, her level of concentration, the presenting problems, and the purpose of the assessment.

In addition to measures of anxiety, questionnaire measures of depression and disruptive behavior problems are valuable adjuncts in the assessment process. The Children's Depression Inventory (CDI; Kovacs 1981) is a specific self-report measure of depressive symptoms in children. It contains twenty-seven items, each consisting of three sentences. Children are required to pick out the sentence that best describes the way they have felt over the past two weeks ("I am sad once in a while," "I am sad many times," "I am sad all the time.") Norms are available for children between six and eighteen years of age. In addition, the Child Behavior Checklist (CBCL; Achenbach 1991) is a useful measure of behavioral problems and competencies in children and adolescents between four and eighteen. For this questionnaire, parents complete 114 items relating to their child's typical reactions and behaviors. The CBCL provides a measure of behaviors across various factors including anxiety, social withdrawal, depression, obsessions-compulsions, noncommunicative behavior, hyperactivity, aggression, and somatic complaints.

Behavioral Measures

As an alternative to structured interviews and self-report measures, there are several forms of behavioral assessment of anxiety in children. These can be useful for younger children who have difficulty reporting their fears due to limited insight or lack of language development. Behavioral measures provide information on the overt aspects of anxiety such as visible distress, crying, tantrums, facial expression, posture, and active avoidance. The two main types of behavioral measures include behavioral avoidance tests and direct observation.

Behavioral avoidance tests involve exposing children to their feared stimuli under controlled conditions and recording information about how they react. For example, if a child had a phobia of dogs, he could be asked to approach a restrained dog in the clinic. Relevant behavioral measures might include closest proximity to the dog, posture, facial expression, and duration of exposure. Younger children often cannot clearly describe their internal experience, but their behaviors show that they are distressed. They may cry, throw a tantrum, freeze, or cling desperately onto major attachment figures when faced with the feared situation. Such tests were popular in the 1960s and 1970s, but they have been used less frequently in recent decades. Behavioral avoidance tests can be impractical to set up in clinic settings and can be difficult to create for many fears that involve a complex set of social and cognitive cues.

Direct observation is a more practical method of behavioral assessment of anxiety in most cases. Direct observation simply involves observation of the overt signs of anxiety in natural settings. The child and family should be observed during the interview, and behavioral aspects such as the child's social skills and reactions to unfamiliar situations should be noted. Specific analogue situations can also be created in the clinic to assess particular features of the child and family. For example, children can be observed interacting with their parents on various tasks to assess parent-child interaction, they can be separated from their parents to assess the response to separation, or other children can be introduced to assess peer-interaction skills.

The primary limitation of behavioral measures is that they are not standardized forms of assessment and are vulnerable to the influence of many extraneous factors. This means that the results cannot be compared across children. In addition, behavioral forms of assessment reveal little about the subjective experience of the anxious child and are probably best used as an adjunct to other forms of assessment. For these reasons behavioral measures are not used as frequently as interviews and questionnaires.

Table 3: Properties of Self-Report Measures of Anxiety in Children

Measure	Subscales	Age Range	Primary Focus	Structure
RCMAS	physiological anxiety, worry/oversensitivity, social concerns/concentration	5–19	chronic anxiety	37 yes/no items
STAIC	A-Trait A-State	9–12	chronic anxiety	20 items on a 3-point scale
FSSC-R	specific fears in several areas: school, home, social, physical, animal, travel, classic phobia, miscellaneous	7–18	specific fears	80 items on a 3-point scale
SPAI-C	assertiveness, traditional social encounters, public performance	8–17	social anxiety	26 items on a 3-point scale
SCAS	separation anxiety, social phobia, obsessive-compulsive disorder, panic-agoraphobia, generalized anxiety, fears of physical injury	8–12	specific symptoms	44 items on a 4-point scale
MASC	physical symptoms, social anxiety, harm avoidance, separation anxiety	8–16	specific symptoms	39 items on a 4-point scale
SCARED	somatic/panic, general anxiety, separation anxiety, social phobia, school phobia	9–18	specific symptoms	38 items on a 3-point scale

Chapter 2

Understanding and Treatment of Anxiety in Children

Demographic Features

Prevalence

Anxiety disorders are the most frequent type of mental disorder in children, just as they are for adults. This is surprising to many clinicians and other professionals who rarely identify or come across these children. Typically, children with anxiety disorders suffer in silence and their parents do not consider the possibility of treatment because the problem is seen as simply part of the child's makeup. But children with these difficulties certainly exist. Whenever we print or air a story about childhood anxiety, we are inundated with inquiries. Some of these children may have been to their primary physician or school counselor, but many have never before sought help from any specialist.

Several epidemiological studies have demonstrated the high frequency of anxiety disorders in children. Two studies, in particular, are worth noting. One was conducted in New Zealand and reported interviews with approximately a thousand fifteen-year-old adolescents and their mothers (Fergusson, Horwood, and Lynskey 1993). Anxiety disorders were the most frequently reported group of disorders by both maternal and child report. When the reports were combined, approximately 10 percent of the group met the *Diagnostic and Statistical*

Manual of Mental Disorders-III-R criteria for at least one anxiety disorder. Similar results were found in an earlier New Zealand study using *DSM-III* criteria and eleven-year-old children (Anderson et al. 1987).

The other noteworthy study examined *DSM-III-R* diagnoses in almost eight hundred thirteen- to eighteen-year-old Dutch adolescents (Verhulst et al. 1997). Again, using either parent or child report, anxiety disorders were by far the most common diagnoses. For example, according to interviews with one parent, over 16 percent of the children met criteria for an anxiety disorder, compared with 3 percent for a mood disorder, 2.5 percent for a disruptive disorder, and 0.4 percent for drug abuse. According to interviews with the child, almost 11 percent met criteria for an anxiety disorder, compared with less than 5 percent for a mood disorder, 7 percent for a disruptive disorder, and 3.5 percent for substance abuse.

Comparisons between the anxiety disorders are more difficult. In our clinic, the most common disorder (as a principal diagnosis) is separation anxiety disorder. Generalized anxiety disorder and social phobia are not far behind. Naturally, age is important in making these comparisons, because separation anxiety disorder is much more common in younger children and social phobia and generalized anxiety disorder are more common in adolescents. In fact, in the Verhulst et al. study social phobia was by far the most common anxiety disorder in that group of adolescents. Specific phobias are very frequent in epidemiological studies. However, in clinical practice they are rarely seen as a principal diagnosis but are very common as additional diagnoses. Obsessive-compulsive disorder is somewhat less frequent than the other anxiety disorders but is seen in a sizable minority. Panic disorder in children of this age group is very rare. We have rarely diagnosed this disorder in children at our clinic and the Verhulst et al. study of adolescents found relatively minor rates according to either parent or child report.

Gender

Anxiety disorders in children appear to be more common in girls than boys, just they they are for adults. For example, in the Fergusson, Horwood, and Lynskey study (1993), anxiety disorders were approximately four times more frequent in girls than in boys. Interestingly, however, this sex difference is not reflected in statistics from our clinic nor from many other specialist child-anxiety centers. In our clinic, we see girls and boys with approximately equal frequency, regardless of age. Clearly, referral practices do not reflect the actual prevalence of these disorders in the community. We can only conclude that parents (who are the main instigators of help-seeking for anxious children) tolerate anxious behaviors more in their daughters than in their sons and boys are therefore being brought in for help at a lower level of anxiety.

Comorbidity

While we regularly talk about a particular child's disorder in singular terms ("the child has a diagnosis of social phobia"), in fact, single disorders are the exception rather than the rule. In general, as discussed in chapter 1, we think about the main disorder that a child has as being the one that seems to interfere most with the child's life. However, in most studies, around 80 percent of children in treatment for one anxiety disorder also meet criteria for at least one other disorder. In most cases, this other disorder is another anxiety disorder.

Table 4: Percentage of Children with Additional Diagnoses across the Various Principal Disorders

Principal Diagnosis	Number of Additional Diagnoses			
	0	1	2	3+
Separation anxiety	10	43	37	10
Social phobia	18	50	25	7
Generalized anxiety	14	48	29	10
Specific phobia	15	58	12	15

Table 5: Average Number of Additional Diagnoses Found across Each of the Principal Disorders

Principal Diagnosis	Total Group	Males	Females	Over 10 Years	Under 9 Years
Separation anxiety	1.5	1.3	1.7	1.8	1.3
Social phobia	1.3	1.1	1.5	1.2	1.4
Generalized anxiety	1.4	1.3	1.3	1.6	1.2
Specific phobia	1.3	1.3	1.3	1.4	1.2

For example, Last, Strauss, and Francis (1987) found that around 75 percent of their sample of anxious children met criteria for more than one *DSM-III* disorder. Early data from our clinic are shown in tables 4 and 5. As you can see, over 80 percent of our children meet *DSM-III-R* criteria for at least one additional disorder and around 40 percent meet criteria for at least two disorders in addition to their principal disorder. The number of additional disorders does not differ greatly between children with various principal diagnoses. Similarly, there is very little difference in comorbidity between boys and girls or between younger and older children. What this tells us is that there is a great deal of overlap and similarity between the various anxiety disorders. There is probably not a great deal of difference in cause and, more importantly, the basic methods of treatment are going to be essentially the same.

Interference

As discussed in the introduction, there is a common misperception that anxiety, when it exists, is not an especially major problem for children. Certainly, there is a widespread assumption that the "serious" childhood problems are depression, externalizing disorders, and substance abuse. We believe that anxiety disorders can in fact produce major interference in a child's life and can result in huge long-term costs to the community.

Anxious children have fewer friends, on average, than other children their age (Rapee and Melville 1997; Strauss et al. 1989). As a result, the development of normal socialization skills and benefits may be delayed. In addition, general peer support and interaction is reduced, putting these kids at higher risk for depression, loneliness, attacks from bullies, and withdrawal. Many of these children are unassertive and therefore tend to have fewer positive experiences and have more frustration in life. Even when anxious children do have several friends, their anxiety may keep them from many social interactions such as dances, going out, school camps, and excursions.

In general, anxious children come from a range of academic backgrounds and abilities. Their overall academic performance is no lower than that for children without anxiety. However, this is possibly due to the tendency for many anxious children to take schoolwork more seriously and put more effort into their work than other children. In fact, their acute academic performance is often affected by anxiety. This is particularly so for pressure or concentration situations, such as exams. We have had many of our parents report to us that their child's schoolwork has improved following treatment at our clinic. Naturally, in the extreme case of school refusal, schoolwork is dramatically affected by anxiety. These children may show disrupted patterns of school attendance, resulting in reduced performance and even the necessity to repeat grades. In extreme cases, these children may not attend school at all for extended periods and will receive schooling at home. Another finding relevant to this issue comes from a study by Phillips and Bruch (1988), which found that shy university students had more restricted career options compared with nonshy students.

Perhaps most of all, anxiety interferes with the general quality of life. Anxious children experience a great deal of personal distress and, while it may be thought of as simply "part of the way they are," it is not necessary. In addition, the anxious behavior can cause considerable disruption to the family. We have had many parents tell us that they have not been able to go out for years because they were not able to leave their child with a sitter or relatives. Similarly, many families describe outings and holidays that were cut short or even canceled due to the child's anxiety.

The long-term prospects for anxious children are also not very good. Certainly, a number of these children will reduce their anxiety over the course of their lives. But a large proportion will very likely go on to have some degree of interference from anxiety throughout their lives. A sizable proportion will continue to have anxiety disorders and develop other problems including depression, drug and alcohol abuse, and suicidal ideation. Two studies are of interest here. First, Caspi, Elder, and Bem (1988) looked at the outcome of shy children (between the ages of eight and ten) over a period of thirty years. They found that those who were most shy as children were also generally the most shy adults. In addition, the males were slower to enter a stable career, get married, and become fathers, and they tended to have lesser occupational achievement and less stable marriages. Females had less of an impact from shyness, but the shy ones were more likely to follow a sexually stereotyped and conservative life course. A second study, by Caspi et al. (1996), examined the psychopathology of twenty-one-year-old adults who previously had been found to have anxious and inhibited temperaments at the age of three. Anxious toddlers were more likely than so called well-adjusted toddlers to develop anxiety, depression, alcohol dependence, and suicidal tendencies in adulthood.

Causes and Maintenance of Anxiety

Any practicing clinician should have a broad understanding of the problems they are dealing with. Having an appreciation for some of the factors that might be involved in the cause or maintenance of anxiety may help you to apply the principles in this program and modify them as needed. Because the main focus of this book is treatment, we don't have the space here to describe a detailed model of the development of anxiety disorders in children, so we will simply cover some of the main principles that we believe are important, especially in the context of treatment. For more detailed accounts, the interested reader should refer to Chorpita and Barlow 1998; Hudson and Rapee in press; Manassis and Bradley 1994; and Rapee in press.

Genetics

There is no doubt that there is a genetic basis to anxiety. Several studies have shown greater concordance for anxiety in monozygotic twins than dizygotic twins and the conclusion from a number of large twin studies is that around 50 percent of the variance in anxious symptoms is genetically determined. In some way, genetic factors are probably involved in almost all types of human behavior. But does this simple fact really tell us anything?

Probably a much more important question than whether genetic factors are involved in the expression of anxiety is the question of what, exactly, is inherited. To begin to answer this question we could look at a study by Torgersen (1983). Torgersen obtained *DSM-III* diagnoses on eighty-five adult pairs of twins: thirty-two monozygotic and fifty-three dizygotic. As expected, when one twin had an anxiety disorder, his or her co-twin was also moderately likely to have an anxiety disorder and this concordance was twice as high for monozygotic twins than for dizygotic twins supporting a genetic basis to anxiety. However, in Torgersen's data, *no two twins had exactly the same disorder.* In other words, if one twin had generalized anxiety disorder, his or her co-twin might have social phobia; if one twin had panic disorder, his or her co-twin might have obsessive-compulsive disorder, and so on. Clearly, then, the genetic basis for anxiety is one that is general to all anxiety disorders and is not specific to particular disorders. In other words, there is no "social phobia gene" or "separation anxiety gene." Rather, there is some genetic involvement that increases a person's chances of developing any anxiety disorder. In fact, more recent research has suggested that this may be an even broader factor labeled by some researchers as a "general neurotic syndrome" (Andrews 1996, 3–20). In other words, what seems to be inherited is the degree to which someone is generally neurotic. Under the right circumstances, this may become manifested as either anxiety disorders or mood disorders (or both).

So it seems, then, that what is inherited is a person's general level of neuroticism. But what does this mean in concrete terms? Most researchers use the term "neuroticism" to refer to the overall level of general emotionality that a person experiences. So what is probably inherited is the general degree to which a person will respond emotionally to various situations—some people are very emotional and some people are quite unemotional. Physiologically, it might be found that people vary in the degree of arousal they experience in response to stressors (Rapee in press).

Temperament

How does a child who is genetically prone to experience anxiety behave? Several researchers have identified a temperamental style that seems to be what we might call an "anxious temperament" in children as young as infancy. One of the most widely accepted patterns has been described by Jerome Kagan of Harvard University, who described a temperamental style that he labeled "behavioral inhibition." Behaviorally inhibited children act in a withdrawn and frightened way in the face of any new or unusual events. They are more prone to cry, cling to their mother, or stare, and less likely to talk, explore, or interact with strangers than other children of their age. Kagan and his colleagues have identified this style of behavior in children as young as a few months and have followed these children over several years. At a few months of age, these children are characterized by increased motor activity and increased crying (similar to descriptions of neurotic people who report being more aroused and emotional). The follow-up research has shown that a large proportion of those children who score in the behaviorally inhibited range at an early age continue to score in this range over later years. This consistency suggests that behavioral inhibition is a true temperament or personality style. Of course, just because behavioral inhibition can be demonstrated in very young children does not prove that it is entirely genetically determined. Even in children a few months of age, environmental factors may be important. But some research has shown that a large part of the variance in behavioral inhibition is genetically determined.

Linking anxious temperament with anxiety disorders in children has been done in several ways. First, some data from our clinic has shown that mothers of children with anxiety disorders report that their children have had several difficulties for a number of years. Compared with nonclinical children, anxious children were reported by their mothers to show more difficult behaviors in infancy, to have more fears in their first two years of life, and to have more difficulty separating from their mothers in their early years (Rapee and Szollos 1997). Second, research from Rosenbaum et al. (1993) has shown that anxious parents are more likely to have children who are behaviorally inhibited and behaviorally inhibited children are more likely to have parents with various anxiety disorders. Finally, children who were behaviorally inhibited at a young age and were followed up over several years were found to be more likely to develop an anxiety disorder than children who were not behaviorally inhibited.

Parenting

What about parents—can they influence their child's anxiety? This is actually a very hard question to answer and the results differ slightly depending on whose perspective one takes. There have been many studies that have given questionnaires to adults with various anxiety disorders and asked them retrospectively about the way their parents handled them. These studies have consistently shown that anxious adults report that their parents were more rejecting and more controlling and overprotective than the parents of nonanxious adults. In general, these results have been more consistent for a controlling parenting style than for a rejecting one. But does this necessarily reflect actual parenting, or could it be more closely related to a biased recall or biased perception of parenting from an anxious perspective?

A few studies have attempted to directly question the parents of anxious offspring about their parenting attitudes and behaviors. These studies have been far less consistent in their results but of course it is very possible that parents may not be honest about their styles of parenting or may not have insight into their reactions. Nevertheless, some of these studies have supported the research from offspring showing that parents of anxious offspring seem to be more rejecting and, in particular, more controlling than other parents.

Finally, from another perspective, we have been looking at the interaction between parents and their children using direct laboratory observations (Hudson and Rapee 1998). In one study, we asked anxious and nonanxious children to complete some complex cognitive tasks. Mothers of the children sat with them while they completed the tasks and were given the answers. They were instructed to help their child *only* if they felt their child really needed it. Raters who didn't know the diagnosis of the child then scored the interactions (from video) on a number of scales. There were several differences between the interactions of anxious children and their mothers versus nonanxious children and their mothers. The most interesting were that mothers of anxious children were more likely to get involved in their child's task and were more likely to offer help when their child did not ask for it. These results support the data from the other perspectives in suggesting that parents of anxious children may be more intrusive, involved, and protective than parents of nonanxious children, particularly at times of difficulty.

Further research at our clinic is beginning to show what any parent could tell you: parents do not treat their kids in the same way. Our parents tell us that they are far more controlling and protective of their anxious child than they are of those of the child's siblings who are not anxious. This suggests that any parenting factors that may be involved in anxiety are not a common factor across a family, but are unique to the particular child who develops an anxiety disorder.

Why would parents become more involved with one child than another? We speculate that it is because a particular child elicits certain responses from their parents. This is very likely given the child's anxious temperament. When an infant or young child is quick to cry or show terror at new things in her life, a parent will understandably respond to the child's distress by becoming more protective and accommodating. This is likely to be even more so if the parent himself is also anxious. In this way, temperamentally anxious children shape their parents' responses to be more protective. But in doing so, these children are not able to learn that the world is not as dangerous as they believe, and their anxiety is maintained.

Cognitive Factors

There is considerable evidence that anxious children have many thoughts concerning dangers and negative outcomes, just as anxious adults do. These thoughts tend to focus on both negative social outcomes ("I will fail," or "They will laugh at me") and negative physical outcomes ("I will get hurt," or "My parents will be killed"). Even more interesting, some evidence suggests that anxious children may interpret ambiguous situations in a threatening way (Barrett et al. 1996). For example, the following scenario was presented to a child: "Imagine that you are walking toward a group of children in school. As you approach, they suddenly begin to laugh. Why do you think they are laughing?" Children who are anxious are more likely to report a threat interpretation such as, "They think I look funny" than are nonanxious children, who are more likely to make a neutral interpretation such as, "Someone just told a joke."

This research suggests that anxious children have internal mental processes that might help make them anxious in various situations. We don't know at this stage whether that is something that comes very early, before they develop a disorder, or whether it is more of a consequence of their anxiety disorder, but once it exists it almost certainly helps maintain the disorder.

Avoidance Behavior

One of the key features of anxiety disorders is avoidance behavior. This behavior may be obvious (such as avoiding school) or it may be subtle (such as avoiding eye contact) but it is a part of the presentation of almost all people with anxiety. In the Barrett et al. (1996) study, kids were asked not only what they would think in the situation, but also what they would do. Children with an anxiety disorder were far more likely to report that they would escape or avoid the situation in some way than nonclinical children and oppositional children. In fact, the avoidance behavior was the strongest differentiator between these groups.

Considerable research has shown that when the fear of a particular object or event is developed, it can be maintained for long periods of time (theoretically indefinitely) if the individual is allowed to avoid the object or event. Conversely, if the individual approaches the object or event, fear can reduce quite quickly. Avoidance or approach behaviors seem to be vital in the maintenance of anxiety.

Other Factors

Several other factors are likely to be involved in the development of anxiety in children. One factor of possible importance is the lessons and messages that the child learns from parents through discussion and observation. This is independent of the way the parent attempts to intentionally shape their child (we have already discussed the role of parenting), but refers to less conscious ways in which the parent influences the child. Much of this influence may come via the child's observations of a parent's manner of acting. If the parent is anxious himself, he will demonstrate to the child anxious ways of responding. He will give the child the message that the world is a dangerous place. Similarly, the parent can impart this type of message (and further enhance their children's anxiety) in a verbal way by agreeing with the child's fearful messages, warning the child of dangers, or paying a lot of attention to threat.

Stressful life events can also reduce feelings of safety in children and increase anxiety. There is considerable research in adults to suggest that many cases of specific phobias are precipitated by a traumatic experience (such as being bitten by a dog). In addition, some types of anxiety, such as post-traumatic stress disorder, are by definition precipitated by major life events. While this is probably not the method by which most cases of chronic anxiety begin, there is little doubt that it may be important in some cases. Further, where conditioning episodes of this type do occur within a background of chronic anxiety, they are certainly likely to exacerbate the anxiety even if they are not the sole or even major cause.

Along similar lines, more general negative life events may exacerbate and maintain anxiety in a child who is temperamentally vulnerable. Some recent data from our clinic showed that children with separation anxiety disorder in particular seemed to have had more negative life events than other children (Rapee and Szollos 1997). In other data from adults with various anxiety disorders, no difference between these adults and nonclinical adults in terms of the simple number of negative events in their lives was found. Rather, the anxious adults seemed to respond to the same types of events with greater distress (Rapee, Litwin, and Barlow 1990). This may suggest that it is not the occurrence of a negative life event per se that precipitates anxiety, but that anxiety may be exacerbated by the reaction to life events in someone who is temperamentally emotional.

An Overall Model

So how do we put all this information together? The complete picture of the development of anxiety is almost certainly a very complex one, but following is a simple model (Rapee in press) of some of the main factors that at least helps us conceptualize where treatment fits in.

According to the model, an anxious parent may produce a child who is born with a vulnerability to anxiety. The specific genetic involvement needs to be delineated through further research, but there is a strong possibility that its main manifestation is via high levels of arousal and emotionality. In turn, the anxious parent is more likely to respond to a vulnerable child with excessive control and protection. The suggestion here is that the parent's basic parenting

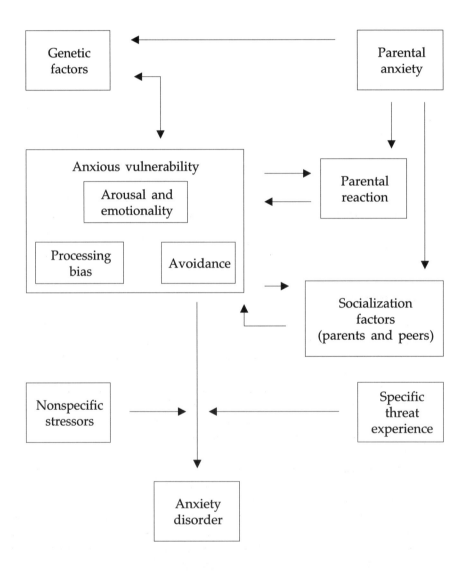

Figure 1: Factors Involved in the Development of Child Anxiety

style is not at "fault." Rather, it is more likely that parents of vulnerable children are responding or reacting to apparent distress in their child. Through the course of many years of dealing with a sensitive and highly aroused child, the parent falls into a maladaptive pattern whereby they anticipate their child's distress and leap to her assistance in order to avoid the expected distress. Avoidance of distress would be even more likely if the parent was herself anxious. Other parental and circumstantial features may also influence the likelihood that a parent will react to an emotional child with overprotection. For example, we have found that clinically anxious children are more likely to have had a birth complication than nonclinical children and are slightly more likely to be first-born (Rapee and Szollos 1997). Either of these factors may influence a parent to be more protective of that child compared with other children in the family. Overprotection provided by the parent is likely to augment the child's vulnerability to anxiety by strengthening tendencies to avoid threat and by increasing the child's tendency to perceive danger and believe that they have no control over danger.

Anxious vulnerability may also be augmented by various social-learning experiences. This may occur via interaction with parents in the early years. Specifically, observational learning and provision of specific information from an anxious parent may enhance the child's tendency to avoid and reinforce the message that the world is a dangerous place and the child lacks any ability to control threat. As with parent reaction, learning from the parent may also interact with an anxious vulnerability. Learning about associations with danger is more rapid in the case of aroused individuals, and processing biases toward threat might also enhance the likelihood of learning about such factors. In later years, anxiety in a child may be maintained and further augmented by acceptance of avoidance behavior and anxious processing through like-minded peers or through rejection and neglect from the mainstream peer group.

The Mechanisms of Treatment

So, based on this model, how can we best treat children who are anxious? Clearly, there is not much we can do about the genetic predisposition, but the other factors can all be altered via the mechanisms described in this book. The central procedures involve helping the child directly modify her anxiety-maintaining factors. Most importantly, the entire cycle of anxiety can be reduced by getting the child to reverse her tendency to avoid threat. The use of exposure is aimed at getting the child to approach feared situations and thereby learn that there is nothing to fear and that she can cope. Teaching the child to think more realistically and reverse the natural tendency to interpret situations as threatening helps this process. In some cases, relaxation techniques can also be useful in helping the child reduce her excessive arousal. In combination with these strategies, we aim to teach parents more constructive methods by which they can help their child. These methods encourage parents to reduce control and to model effective coping. Finally, additional strategies such as social-skills training and assertiveness training help the child reduce negative experiences and increase the likelihood that her interactions will be positive.

Treatment Outcome Research

At least three studies have been conducted to empirically test the value of these types of procedures in the reduction of broad-based anxiety disorders in children. The first study was conducted by Phillip Kendall at Temple University in Philadelphia (1994). Forty-seven anxious children were randomly allocated to either treatment or a wait list. Treatment was based on the "Coping Cat Workbook" (Kendall 1992) and involved 16 sessions, largely with the child alone. Compared to those on the wait list, the active treatment produced a highly significant decrease in anxiety as measured by both parent and child reports. Approximately 64 percent of the treated children no longer met full criteria for a *DSM-IV* diagnosis at the end of treatment, compared with 5 percent of the children on the wait list. These results were maintained at the one year follow-up.

Barrett, Dadds, and Rapee (1996) conducted an extension of the Kendall study. Seventy-nine anxious children were randomly allocated to one of three groups: a wait list (as a control), a child-alone treatment, and a family treatment. The child-alone treatment was based closely on Kendall's program except that it was reduced to twelve sessions. The family treatment involved identical procedures to the child-alone treatment but also involved the parents as active participants in the program and taught them child-management strategies. Results showed that, as for Kendall's study, the child-alone program produced significantly greater reductions in anxiety than that produced by the wait list. However, the family treatment resulted in even better results. At the end of treatment, 84 percent of the family group no longer met full criteria for a *DSM-IV* diagnosis compared with 57 percent of the child-alone group and 26 percent of the wait list. Results were maintained and even slightly greater at one year follow-up.

Finally, in our more recent treatment program we have continued the strategy of including parents in treatment. We have slightly modified our program from the one at the University of Queensland by further reducing it to nine sessions (over eleven weeks), removing the relaxation component (to allow the shorter program), and conducting treatment in groups of five to seven families. Our data from the first seventy-five families was excellent (Rapee 1996). There was a marked reduction in anxiety at posttreatment according to reports from both the parents and children that was equal to what was achieved in Queensland, and the improvements continue up to the one-year follow-up. The results based on both the mother's report and the child's report are shown below.

Not only have excellent results been shown in university-based research programs, but we have also shown that we can successfully apply our program in a hospital-based outpatient clinic. Recent results have demonstrated that conducting treatment for anxious children within a general child and adolescent psychiatry unit results in an outcome similar to that of our university program (Wignall and Rapee 1998). We have also developed a condensed version of the program that is conducted over a single intensive week and is therefore suitable for children from rural and remote regions. This program also seems to produce excellent success (Kowalenko et al. 1998).

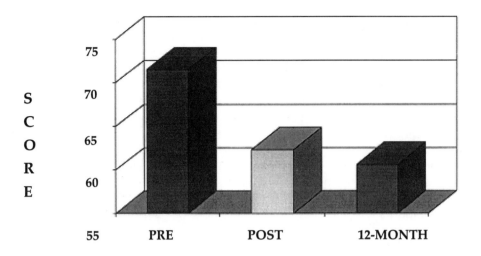

Figure 2: Changes in Scores on Mother's Report of Her Child's Anxiety (CBCL-internalizing) at the Macquarie University Program

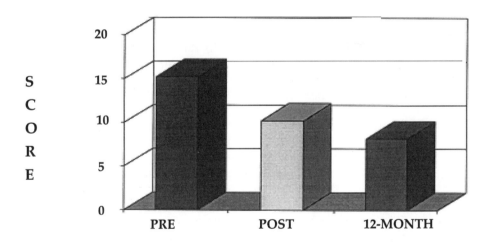

Figure 3: Changes in Scores on the Child's Report of Anxiety (RCMAS) at the Macquarie University Program

So, the results from several studies show that we can successfully reduce anxiety in a large proportion of children who come for treatment of their anxiety disorder. Are there any factors that can help us predict which children are less likely to be helped? We have tried to look at a number of possible predictors of treatment outcome from our data at Macquarie. The first point to make is that very few of the obvious factors seem to make any difference. Children improve in response to treatment regardless of the degree of additional externalizing problems they have, regardless of their parents' levels of depression, and regardless of how credible their parents view the program to be at the beginning. Age and sex also have little effect—both boys and girls and younger children and adolescents improve to much the same degree. Diagnosis also has little influence in the longer term. What we find is that separation anxiety disorder seems to respond to treatment a little quicker than the others. Therefore, at post-treatment, children with separation anxiety disorder as their principal disorder tend to do better than the others. However, by the one-year follow-up, children with principal diagnoses of social phobia and generalized anxiety disorder have caught up and all are doing equally well.

Though marital satisfaction is possibly one factor to watch out for, it is not nearly as important as one might expect. We have had several families in treatment who were in the process of separating and yet were able to put aside their differences to help their child. In such cases, marital distress has no effect on treatment. Only when couples are unable to put aside their differences is treatment likely to be compromised. The data back up this conjecture: we find that measures of marital distress are only slightly correlated with poor outcome.

Clearly, there is still a great deal to learn about the nature of anxiety in children. In addition, treatment is not a hundred percent effective so we are always searching for improvements. But it is also clear that we currently have a highly effective treatment for childhood anxiety disorders that works for the vast majority of children. It is efficient (it can be run in groups) and flexible (it works in various formats and can be run by therapists from a range of backgrounds). The following chapters will describe the components of the program in detail. We will begin by introducing some cases that will be used throughout the book to illustrate the procedures.

Chapter 3

Case Studies

This chapter presents several case studies to give you a richer understanding of anxiety-disordered children and their families. Clearly, the difficulties that anxious children experience are heterogeneous and idiosyncratic; no two children will present *exactly* the same pattern. However, these case studies should provide you with a broad appreciation of some of the ways in which such children and parents present the disorder(s). In particular, the studies highlight the importance of a thorough assessment of both the child and the family to identify the range of problems experienced. We will refer to these cases throughout the book to illustrate particular applications of our treatment program.

Jessica

Twelve-year-old Jessica's parents report that she worries about "everything and anything." They report she is troubled by new situations and events out of her normal routine. According to her parents, she worries about situations two weeks before they occur. Before school every morning, Jessica complains of feeling sick in her stomach. At school, she reports that she worries about getting hurt, making mistakes, being late, and getting into trouble. Her parents report that Jessica is constantly asking for reassurance in situations and will ask many "what if?" questions. They also report that she becomes fearful when she hurts herself. She will yell and scream and worry that she has hurt herself severely. Often, the worries center around the possibility that she has broken a bone. Jessica has two younger siblings and she also worries about their safety. She often keeps an eye on them around the house to make sure they do not hurt themselves.

Jessica's parents describe her as a perfectionist. She works very hard at school and always completes her homework as soon as she arrives home. Her work is very neat and she will often attempt homework pages several times before she is satisfied.

Jessica has difficulties getting to sleep and will often take up to an hour and a half before falling asleep. She explains that this time is spent worrying about the day that has passed and also about the events of the following day. Jessica and her parents report that she is also highly concerned about burglars and is afraid that someone will break into the house and hurt her. When she hears a noise outside, she insists that her mother investigate.

According to her parents, Jessica is also fearful of needles and avoids going to the doctor as much as she can for that reason. Her parents have had to drag her to the doctors even on occasions when she has been very ill, and whenever she has to have a needle she will scream and cry.

Her parents report that Jessica has a strong desire to be liked. They describe her as a timid child and they believe she would have difficulties answering a question in class because she would be frightened of making a mistake and being embarrassed. Jessica reports that she sometimes worries about what other children think of her. According to her parents, whenever she greets people she does not use eye contact and often mumbles when she speaks. She has been able to make speeches in front of the class but reported feeling quite nervous. She has several friends at school whom she occasionally sees outside school hours. After an initial warm-up period, she does not usually have a great deal of trouble making friends.

Jessica meets criteria for a principal diagnosis of generalized anxiety disorder and an additional diagnosis of specific phobia, blood-injury type. In addition Jessica experiences some mild social anxiety, although it is not intrusive enough to warrant a diagnosis.

Sally

Sally is a seven-year-old girl whose parents report that she has always had difficulties separating from them. She reports feeling "funny in the tummy" prior to school, at after-school activities, and at parties. In the time leading up to these events, Sally and her parents report that she will worry and ask questions about where her parents will be and when they will be picking her up. During separation, she will often scream and cry and cling to her mother. Her mother reports that at home Sally will frequently follow her around the house, try to play in whatever room her Mom is in, and will often try to engage her in conversation. Sally has had extreme difficulties attending school and in the last year has missed over twenty days. Almost every morning before school she cries and becomes very distressed. Sally's teacher has been involved in assisting her in getting to class. Each morning before school, her mother has to drag her out of the car to meet the teacher at the gate. From there both Sally's mother and the teacher escort her to the classroom. This procedure is not always successful because Sally either refuses to get into the car at home or refuses to get out of the car once at school. On occasion Sally refuses to go to school at all and her mother is forced to stay at home with her, as no alternative care arrangements are available.

Sally's parents report that she does not attend any activities outside of school that her mother cannot attend with her. Recently, she wanted to begin ballet classes, but when she realized her mother could not stay with her she refused to attend. Sally will often have friends over to visit at her own house, but will not go out to play at other people's houses. She has never stayed at a friend's or relative's house overnight without either of her parents. Sally does not like being in crowded situations because she is fearful she will get lost. Her parents report that she is very clingy in these situations. Sally revealed that she often has nightmares about her parents being in a car accident or being taken by "a robber." She also reports that she worries about "something bad" happening to her mother. In addition to her main concerns, Sally also worries about dogs, spiders, and the dark.

Sally meets criteria for a principal diagnosis of separation anxiety disorder and an additional diagnosis of specific phobia, animal type.

Simon

Simon is fifteen years old. His mother reports that he has always been a shy child and has never had many friends, even in preschool. In agreement, Simon reports that he has only one or two friends at school but has very little contact with these boys outside of school. According to Simon, he does not like going to parties or going out with his friends. If he does go out to parties, he reports that he likes to have a few alcoholic drinks to feel more comfortable. He says he constantly worries about what other people are thinking of him. He states that he is concerned that people will think he is stupid or uncool. His mother reports that he always insists on having his clothes "just right." Even in winter Simon does not like to wear long sleeves because he sweats easily and then worries that people will notice he is sweating.

Simon reports that he becomes extremely nervous if he is required to give a speech in front of the class and will skip school to avoid this. His mother and the school have become concerned about his school attendance because he is often truant. Even catching the school bus is difficult, so Simon prefers to walk or be driven.

He also reports feeling very depressed at times. His mother states that sometimes he will mope around the house for periods that last several days to weeks. Simon reports that he has very little confidence in himself and feels that he is "hopeless" at school and at making friends. He dislikes recess and lunch because he has to find a way to pass the time without talking to people too much. When he feels down, he finds it difficult to focus on his work and this adds to his dislike of school. He states that when he gets depressed he sometimes thinks he "does not have much to live for," although he says he has not seriously considered committing suicide. Simon says he often does not get to sleep until late (midnight or one) and will wake at six for school. He says that he has too much on his mind and just can't get to sleep, but because he doesn't get much sleep he feels really tired and lethargic during the day. Simon's mother also reports that recently he has become more irritable at home and has been having a lot more fights with his younger brother. Importantly, both Simon and his parents report that, at the moment, his mood is not too bad and it is his social fears that are the most pressing problem. (If Simon's mood had been especially poor—including extreme lethargy, low motivation, and hopelessness, or if he had active suicidal thoughts—his depression would have to be dealt with before much attention could be paid to the social concerns.)

Simon's parents have been separated for five years and divorced for eighteen months. Simon sees his father every second weekend and spends roughly half of the school holidays with him. According to Simon's mother, his father does not believe Simon has a problem and believes it is all a normal part of growing up. His mother reports that Simon's father has told her she is worrying about nothing and he will grow out of it.

Simon meets criteria for a principal diagnosis of social phobia and an additional diagnosis of major depressive disorder.

Jason

Jason is a nine-year-old boy whose presenting complaint is a concern about germs. According to Jason and his parents, he constantly worries about whether he has germs on his hands and whether he will become sick and die as a result. He reports that in order to prevent these germs from making him sick, he washes his hands frequently. Before and after going to the toilet Jason will spend at least five minutes washing his hands. He will wash again, for similar periods of time, before and after meals and whenever he perceives his hands as being dirty. He says that he does not avoid playing outside where he may get dirty but will make frequent trips to the bathroom to wash his hands. According to his mother, Jason will also often change his clothes during his play if they become dirty. She says he has a shower or a bath two to three times a day and will become distressed and teary if this is not possible. Jason reports feeling "funny" or "weird" in his stomach when he thinks he may be dirty. His hands have often become very sore and dry due to the frequent washing and at one stage his parents took him to a skin specialist for treatment. His parents estimate that he spends roughly two hours a day washing.

At school, Jason avoids using the toilets because he believes they are full of germs. He will, however, make frequent use of the sinks in the bathroom. Jason is very neat both at school and at home and insists that his school uniform be clean and pressed every day. He becomes distressed if his hair is not neat or his clothes are not as he wants them. His handwriting is precise and his desk and room are always tidy. Jason reports that he is teased a lot at school, particularly about his tidiness. Although his parents report that he has always been tidy and clean, they say that this problem worsened when he started school at the age of five. They also report a worsening of symptoms in the last six months.

According to his parents, Jason is pedantic about what he eats. He insists on inspecting every mouthful of food for germs and "off" bits. He refuses to eat food if he has been unable to observe its preparation and will thus usually refuse to eat at locations other than home.

Jason's parents report that over the past nine months they have been experiencing difficulties in their marriage. They have also been in disagreement regarding the management of Jason's problematic behavior. His mother feels she is not getting adequate support from her husband in terms of the difficulties she is experiencing with Jason. His father says he does not agree with the way his wife is handling Jason's difficulties; he thinks she fusses over him too much, so he tends to stand back and not get involved.

Jason meets criteria for a principal diagnosis of obsessive-compulsive disorder.

Chapter 4

Getting Started

At the commencement of any treatment program it is essential to build within your client a feeling of confidence, hope, and encouragement. They are about to embark on a long course of hard work and tough challenges, and treatment will have a reduced chance of succeeding if they are not highly motivated. For this reason, it is very worthwhile to put time and effort into increasing motivation.

Motivation can be improved in various ways. Most simply, people will be more motivated when they feel a strong connection with their therapist, when they feel confidence in their therapist's knowledge and ability, and when they have a good understanding of the nature of their problem and the goals and expectations of treatment. For this reason, in the first session, it is important to build rapport, to explain the nature of the treatment program, and to help your client to gain an understanding of their problems and how the treatment program will address those problems.

Given the interactive patterns in many anxious families, it is not uncommon for one parent to take over and do all of the talking for the child. We have experienced situations in which every time we asked the child a question, the parent answered. Kindly but firmly letting the parent know that you want the child to answer can provide the beginning of therapy—teaching the parent to let his child fend for herself (there's more on this topic in chapter 7). For younger children, you may only expect them to answer a few simple questions to begin with (depending on their degree of anxiety) and it may be quite appropriate for the parents to help in many aspects. For adolescents, you would generally aim most of the questions and comments toward them and you would expect little help from the parents. In fact, with older or more mature adolescents, you may conduct little therapy at all with the family group together, especially in the early stages. Again, it is important to let adolescents know that you respect their individuality and that you see them as an equal.

In the group situation, this component of treatment is even more important. Of course, the importance of confidentiality and other group rules must be discussed before this process begins (see the appendix for a thorough discussion of group treatment). We usually take at least half of the first session to get each family to describe their situation. While you need to be careful that the parents don't embarrass their children, getting each family to describe their child's difficulty is a great way to help the kids realize that they are not alone and that they have things in common with other members of the group. Often, parents are also greatly relieved to realize that there are other parents who have had to deal with the limitations that anxiety causes. In order to limit the degree of disclosure that occurs without the child's approval in front of her peers, we generally ask families to simply describe the main, broad problems that the child has and encourage the child to do the talking if she is willing. We then continue the discussion with the parents alone once the children have left the room.

With a group of anxious children without their parents, silence can be a common difficulty. If the silence is not too extreme, we will simply proceed with the first session and the children will usually relax with time. However, in severe cases, we will spend much of the first session or more playing games. Forming the kids into teams is usually a great way to get them to interact.

Again, the goals of treatment need to be discussed with both the parents and the child during this first session. The following points should be covered:

- You are not there to take away the child's fears.

- Instead, you will help teach techniques and strategies by which the child can learn to master his fears.

- At the end of formal therapy, the child will only be partly improved. Learning new skills takes time and considerable improvement will occur over the coming years after therapy is finished.

- Ultimately, the goal is not to make the child "anxiety-free." Rather, the aim is to help the child master his anxiety so that it no longer interferes with his life.

Recognizing Feelings, Symptoms, and Thoughts

The first stage of treatment is to ensure that the child understands the nature of feelings, thoughts, and symptoms. This is especially important for younger children who often have very little understanding of how their thoughts, feelings, and symptoms fit together. For adolescents, we usually go through this information very briefly and then cover a brief, age-appropriate version of the nature of anxiety that is covered with parents (covered below under Why Are Some People Anxious?).

Feelings

The first step is to make sure that kids can describe the differences between various emotional states. We usually show children under nine years a series of pictures of various facial expressions and ask them to tell us what the particular emotion is. Some examples appear in figure 4, below. You might also ask the child to make faces that indicate various emotions. This can be turned into a game: write a range of different emotions onto pieces of paper and ask the child to select the pieces from a container that match that expression. Small rewards such as a sweet or a sticker should be given for good attempts. This type of exercise works even better in a group format.

For slightly older young children or early adolescents (say, ten to fourteen), this type of game may be too simplistic. Instead, we might get them to brainstorm "feeling words" and put these on a board. It is a good idea to draw connections between various events and feelings. For example, "Tell me as many words as you can to say how you would feel if you lost your wallet . . . if you were being chased by an angry dog . . . if you got the top mark in your exam . . ." and so on.

As part of the discussion of feelings, introducing children and parents to the notion of quantifying their feelings can have a number of advantages. Most importantly, it helps children realize that their feelings are not just random events that happen all at once but that their feelings vary depending on the nature of the situation. Learning to think in terms of the intensity of their anxiety is a very important aspect of most of the techniques outlined later in this book, because during most strategies, children will be asked to rate their levels of anxiety. You can begin by showing the child a scale from zero to ten (see figure 5) in which different levels of anxiety and worry are indicated, then lead a brief discussion in which the different levels of anxiety are placed into context by referring to various anxiety-provoking situations. For example, "How anxious would you be jumping out of a plane . . . seeing a medium-sized dog . . . seeing a large spider . . . ?" and so on.

Symptoms

At this stage, the aim is to get kids to realize the types of physical feelings that are connected with anxiety. For younger children, a fun exercise is to ask them to think about what happens to animals when they are frightened. A discussion about the changes they can witness in a frightened cat is a good start. Younger children should be encouraged to come up with changes such as fur standing on end, big eyes, shaking, a scared expression, fast breathing, and so on. After thinking about animals, children should then think about the changes that occur in their own bodies when they are feeling worried or nervous. An alternate exercise that works well for younger children (and can also be fun for adolescents) is to give them an outline of a human body and ask them to mark all the different places that are affected when they feel anxious (see figure 6). Many kids turn this into a fun exercise by being very artistic. An even more fun way of doing this is to get a large sheet of butcher paper, ask the child to lie on

How are you feeling today?

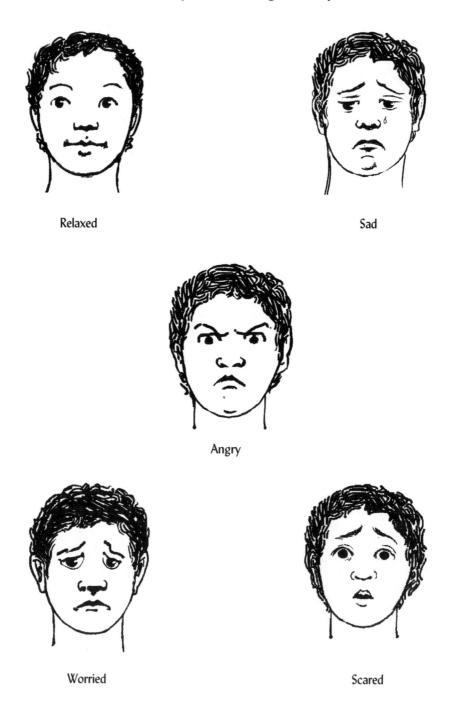

Relaxed

Sad

Angry

Worried

Scared

Figure 4: Labeling Different Feelings

How are you feeling today?

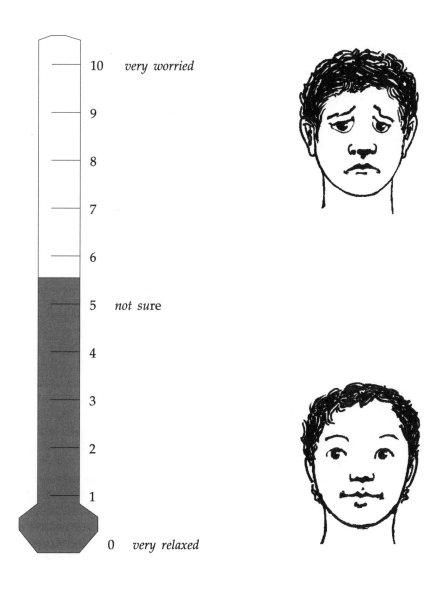

10   *very worried*

9

8

7

6

5   *not sure*

4

3

2

1

0   *very relaxed*

Figure 5: Worry Scale

it, and then trace around their body with a pen. She can then use this picture of herself to indicate where she is affected by anxiety. Some adolescents may consider this drawing childish (although many adults in our training workshops enjoy doing it!). If this is the case, simply ask the adolescent to brainstorm all the ways in which anxiety affects him physically. You should then describe any additional typical symptoms that haven't been covered.

Thoughts

The best way to get younger children to discuss the types of thoughts they have during anxiety is to illustrate the links between situations, thoughts, and feelings. This is the precursor to cognitive restructuring.

Begin by providing a couple of examples of different situations and then ask the child to indicate possible thoughts and feelings. For example, "Imagine that you are taking a test in class and you look across and see the person next to you looking at your work. What would you think? How would you feel?" "Imagine that you get home and your mother tells you that you are going away next weekend for a holiday to the beach. What would you think? How would you feel?"

You can then use these examples to illustrate that different thoughts are associated with different feelings. Next, you need to illustrate the point that there is not always a single thought and feeling for each given situation. In other words, sometimes some situations are confusing and how you feel will depend on what you think. Once again, illustrate this with examples: "Imagine that you are giving a talk to the class and some children at the back begin to giggle. What might you think? How would you feel? Now try to think of a different thought you could have. How might you feel then?" "Imagine that a kid comes up to you in the playground and tells you that the principal is looking for you. What would you think? How would you feel? Now try to think of a different thought you could have. How might you feel then?"

In each case, one would expect an anxious child to come up with a negative thought the first time ("Something is wrong at home") and they should feel bad. The second time, they will hopefully come up with a more neutral or even positive thought ("Mom has come to take me home early") and they should feel neutral or happy. If they come up with these thoughts in the reverse order (neutral first, anxious second), that is not a problem for the sake of the exercise. If the child is having difficulty coming up with thoughts, some prompting may be needed. The point to be illustrated to children is that the type of thought we have in a situation can vary and what we think can change how we feel.

As an alternative to the hypothetical situations above, you can also illustrate this point through the use of ambiguous pictures (see sample exercise 1).

Why Are Some People Anxious?

Parents will have a number of questions and concerns about their child's anxiety: "Why is my child like this? Why one child and not the other? What have I

Instructions: Circle or draw an arrow to changes that happen in your body when you are nervous.

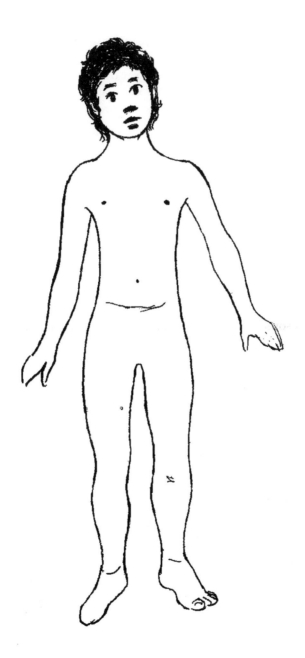

Figure 6: How Does My Body Feel When I Am Worried?

done wrong?" Similarly, older adolescents may have concerns about why they are anxious and how treatment is going to help them. For this reason, in the first session, we discuss with older adolescents and parents some of the facts and figures of anxiety.

Basically, the information we give out in this session covers much of what was discussed in chapter 2 and to some extent also the diagnostic information in chapter 1. This information must, of course, be slightly simplified and tailored for the layperson and even more simplified for older adolescents. The information you need to impart to the parents and older adolescents should fulfill three main purposes:

- reduce guilt, confusion, and embarrassment

- provide an understanding of their problem and the possibility and limitations of change

- provide a framework for treatment to increase credibility and motivation

The sort of information that we cover typically includes:

- a description of the symptoms and features of anxiety

- a description of the different manifestations and types of anxiety disorders

- discussion of the normality of anxiety and its evolutionary adaptiveness

- discussion of the genetics of anxiety, pointing out the limitations of change

- discussion of the factors that maintain anxiety

- discussion of the ways in which the treatment program will address each of the maintaining factors

Keeping Records

As in most structured-treatment programs, make sure that your clients (both child and parent) keep regular records about a number of issues. Such self-monitoring is useful for several reasons: it is a prompt for people to complete various practice exercises, it helps develop insight into a person's problem and increase objectivity, it spells out the details of an exercise and increases the learning that comes from it, and it helps identify triggers and possible causes for problems. We strongly recommend that you include recording as part of your child's practice each week.

At the end of each chapter, we provide a description of the exercises that your child and his parents should be practicing between sessions. In most cases, we have also included forms to go with these exercises. Most of these forms are also reproduced in our parent's manual. You may wish to use these forms as they are printed here, or in some cases you may want to modify them slightly to fit better with your child's idiosyncrasies.

Self-talk 1: Seeing a big dog in the street

Self-talk 2: Mom is home late

Sample Exercise 1: Different Types of Thoughts

Self-talk 3:   Your teacher asks you to give a talk to the class

Self-talk 4:   Meeting other kids

Sample Exercise 1: Different Types of Thoughts (continued)

Clients will do self-monitoring to the extent that they see it as a valuable part of therapy. Therefore, you will need to carefully explain the purpose and value of monitoring to the child and his parents. As with all exercises, adolescents can be expected to make sure that they do their recording themselves. Younger children will need more prompting and help from parents. In addition, you will need to make sure that you spend the beginning of each therapy session going over the practice exercises that the child was expected to do since the previous session. Your failure to do this will very quickly give the message to the child that practice and monitoring are not really important, and his efforts will consequently fade quickly.

Practice

Following the discussion of the link between thoughts and feelings, the homework for this section of the program involves children spending some time keeping a record of their anxious thoughts and feelings. The two forms we use are shown in sample exercise 2 (for the adolescent) and sample exercise 3 (for the younger child).

These exercises require children to choose a time when they felt worried during the day and record: (a) the situation, (b) their thoughts about the situation, (c) the resultant feeling, and (d) their overall level of anxiety on a scale of zero to ten. This should be done whenever the child feels anxious, at least once each day. Children should be encouraged to leave a blank copy of the exercise somewhere obvious (such as by the bed or on their desk) so that they remember to do it every day. Ask parents to remind their younger children to fill it out, and encourage adolescents to ask for reminders from their parents if they think they could use them. Remember, if you ask your client to do this exercise, you must follow up the next week and give lots of praise for successful completion. This is a valuable exercise because it starts to get the child thinking about how their anxiety varies and what sorts of differences (especially different thoughts) go along with the different levels of worry.

Dealing with Difficulties

It is not uncommon for children to have some difficulty with the concepts of thoughts and feelings and, in particular, to confuse the two. In most cases, continued practice will help the child grasp the concepts. For practice in labeling thoughts, children can be given worksheets with cartoon characters in various situations and be asked to guess what the character might be thinking. Thought bubbles are helpful because many children are used to seeing thoughts written in this way for cartoon characters. Similarly, if a child is unclear about the concept of feelings, additional work will be needed defining and labeling feelings in themselves and others. If the child has a great deal of trouble with these concepts, therapy should proceed nonetheless because many children can continue fruitfully without fully being able to use the traditional language.

Linking thoughts and feelings

What happened? _____

What was I thinking? _____

_____

What was I feeling? _____
Worry Scale

```
< 0   1   2   3   4   5   6   7   8   9   10 >
```

What happened? _____

What was I thinking? _____

_____

What was I feeling? _____
Worry Scale

```
< 0   1   2   3   4   5   6   7   8   9   10 >
```

What happened? _____

What was I thinking? _____

_____

What was I feeling? _____
Worry Scale

```
< 0   1   2   3   4   5   6   7   8   9   10 >
```

Sample Exercises 2: Linking Thoughts and Feelings

Learning about my thoughts and feelings

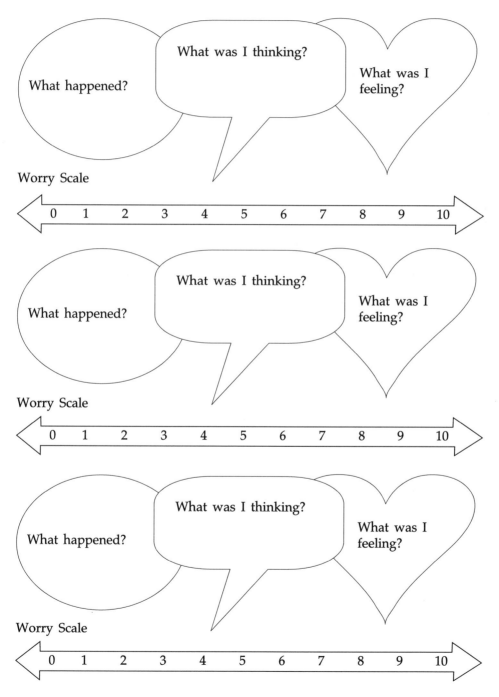

Sample Exercises 3: Linking Thoughts and Feelings

Chapter 5

Cognitive Restructuring

As we described in chapter 2, anxious children are more likely than nonanxious children to see the world as threatening or dangerous. Clearly, changing these perceptions is the main, underlying principle of treatment. Cognitive restructuring is the first step toward changing these beliefs.

Treatment-outcome studies with anxious adults have consistently shown that changes in unrealistic patterns of thinking are a good predictor of improvement in anxiety symptoms (Foa et al. 1996). Fewer comparative studies with children and adolescents exist, but the literature to date indicates that cognitive restructuring is an effective component in the treatment of anxiety disorders in youth (Barrett, Dadds, and Rapee 1996).

The type of cognitive restructuring that we use is based on the work of Aaron Beck (1976). This approach involves changing unrealistic thoughts by examining, in a highly structured fashion, the evidence for these thoughts. The steps can be learned by rote and then applied in everyday situations so that the child is able to handle her anxiety without the aid of the therapist. This provides a lifelong skill that the child can draw upon to cope with various negative emotions over the years.

In some cases the concepts involved in this type of cognitive restructuring are just too complex for children to fully grasp, due to less developed cognitive or verbal skills or a lack of insight. Children who really struggle with understanding this technique of cognitive restructuring typically do better with self-instructional training based on the work of Donald Meichenbaum (1977). (This simpler technique is briefly described later in this chapter under Dealing with Difficulties.)

The therapist begins cognitive restructuring by introducing the rationale and basic techniques of challenging thoughts, and then works through many examples in subsequent sessions. Children and adolescents usually take several sessions to properly understand the technique, and require guidance and frequent practice both in and out of sessions. Typically several core beliefs or interpretations related to the child's primary anxiety will emerge over time and will require increased attention. Parents must be given a thorough understanding of cognitive restructuring so that they are equipped to assist their child with practice and can use the technique for their own anxiety if necessary. On this point, you need to be aware of the powerful impact of parental anxiety, via mechanisms such as modeling and maladaptive styles of thinking, and be on the lookout for these influences (see chapter 7).

Introducing the Rationale for Cognitive Restructuring

Both children and their parents are taught cognitive restructuring. In applying the technique, we generally use the term "realistic thinking" when talking with parents and adolescents and "worried thinking" and "calm thinking" when talking with younger children. The rationale we provide parents is that by learning to apply realistic thinking to their own lives, they will be in the best position to teach it to their children. However, a somewhat hidden purpose of teaching the strategy directly to parents is to help them work on their own fears and worries and model this to their children. As for most of the techniques in this program, parents and children are taught separately. However, for younger children, keeping the parents in the room while teaching cognitive restructuring to the child is useful in that the therapist can model to the parents ways of applying the technique to their child.

Parents and Adolescents

Both parents and adolescents, especially older adolescents, can be given very similar instructions in the explanation of cognitive restructuring. Generally, it's best to begin with an example in which an ambiguous event occurs. One good example for adults is, "Imagine that your partner is late getting home from work." They should be asked to indicate their immediate emotional reaction. You could then continue by suggesting, "Now imagine that you suddenly remembered that your partner told you they had a meeting and would be home late—how would you feel then?"

Adolescents should be given a similar, relevant example such as, "Imagine that you had arranged to meet a new date at six o'clock and he was not there at a quarter past six." Then, "Suddenly you remember that you got the time wrong and you were actually supposed to meet at half past six." Such examples illustrate the principle that feelings are not always directly produced by external circumstances. Rather, our thoughts, beliefs, and attitudes mediate how we feel about an event. Further, the point needs to be made that extreme emotions (such as excessive anxiety) are usually mediated by extreme and unrealistic beliefs. If these beliefs can be slightly reduced and made more realistic, the emotion (anxiety) will also be slightly reduced.

You should also go on to outline the two cognitive biases most commonly displayed by anxious individuals: the tendency to overestimate how likely it is that unpleasant events will happen, and the tendency to overestimate how bad the consequences will be if the event does happen. This point may be familiar to them from the earlier discussion of the causes of anxiety. If not, examples are a useful way to get across the message. For example, an adolescent with high social anxiety when presenting a speech may believe that it is highly probable that they will make large mistakes in their presentation, and this would result in everyone laughing at them. In this example, both the probability and the cost of the feared event are most likely overestimates.

One final point should be made with parents and older adolescents (but is generally not necessary with younger children). When introducing cognitive restructuring, some people will assume you are talking about positive thinking. It is necessary to point out that cognitive restructuring is about thinking *realistically*, rather than about thinking positively. At times life is very difficult, and it is normal and okay to feel upset, angry, or anxious. The aim of cognitive restructuring is not to encourage people to try to think positively all the time, but rather to modify extreme emotions by changing extreme, unrealistic beliefs. Cognitive restructuring will only be effective if the individual can truly believe what they are saying to themselves. It is usually easier to believe realistic thoughts than it is to believe overly positive thoughts.

Younger Children

Naturally, younger children will require a more simplified explanation of cognitive restructuring than will adolescents and parents. However, they can often be much easier to convince and are often very good at applying the principles.

The rationale for cognitive restructuring can be introduced by reminding the child of the way in which thoughts are associated with emotions (as discussed in the previous chapter). In particular, the child should be reminded of an ambiguous situation in which he or she could have different thoughts associated with different feelings. For example, "It is dark and there is a noise outside—what do you think it might be?" The important point to make is that though the situation did not change, the different ways of thinking about the noise outside led to different feelings.

The following points should be made to younger children:

- Our feelings come directly from the things that we think.

- When faced with a situation, we can have different types of thoughts, some of which make us feel more worried than others.

- When we become anxious, it is because we are expecting bad things to happen.

- The types of thoughts we have when we feel anxious are called "worried thoughts."

- The types of thoughts we have when we do not feel anxious are called "calm thoughts."

- If we can change worried thinking to calm thinking, we will feel less anxious.

- It is not easy to change the way we think, because we have usually been thinking this way for a long time, and these thoughts come so fast that we may not notice them. However, with lots of practice, it is possible to change worried thoughts over time.

Introducing the Steps of Cognitive Restructuring

Having introduced the rationale of cognitive restructuring, the next phase of treatment introduces the steps involved in thinking realistically. In brief, these include: (a) identifying the thought behind the emotion, (b) looking for evidence for the thought, (c) evaluating the thought on the basis of the evidence, and (d) examining the consequences of the feared event (the latter is only relevant to parents and older adolescents).

Step 1: Identifying the Thought behind the Emotion

The first step in cognitive restructuring involves identifying the thought behind the negative emotion. At first, this may seem difficult for many children as well as their parents due to the automatic nature of thoughts and the lack of insight in some younger children. Your previous work with the child in which you looked at different types of thoughts has hopefully given them some initial practice at generating and identifying thoughts. We have found that children and adolescents are best able to identify unrealistic thoughts by asking themselves one or more questions such as, "What is making me feel scared?", "What am I worried will happen?" and "What bad thing am I expecting to happen in this situation?" The critical task in step 1 is to identify the unpleasant event the child expects to happen in a particular situation. We recommend describing these thoughts consistently with a standard phrase such as "worried thoughts," because that will help maintain clarity for children. Some common negative predictions reported by children across the most common anxiety disorders are listed in table 6.

Table 6: Common Worried Thoughts across the Anxiety Disorders

Anxiety Disorder	Worried Thoughts
Separation anxiety disorder	"Mom will get hurt in a bad accident and will not come back."
Social phobia	"I will do something stupid and everyone will laugh at me."
Generalized anxiety disorder	"I will fail the test."
Obsessive-compulsive disorder	"I am contaminated with germs and will get sick."

There are two general guidelines to follow when identifying unrealistic thoughts. The first is that the thought should be phrased in the form of a statement. What is needed is a clear statement of what the child is expecting to occur in a given situation. Anxious children will sometimes report their thoughts in the form of a question, such as, "I wonder if I will pass this math test?" The difficulty with phrasing a thought as a question is that it is probably not an accurate reflection of the true cognition underlying the extreme emotion. As noted previously, extreme negative emotions typically follow from extreme negative predictions, and are unlikely to arise through a more vague questioning of possible outcomes. The thought that is more likely to be underlying the anxiety in the math-test example is something such as, "I am going to fail this math test." This thought can be worked with by examining the evidence that they will in fact fail. Therefore, it is important to identify the unpleasant expectation in terms of a specific, clear statement.

The second guideline in identifying extreme beliefs is to avoid having emotions as the theme of the negative prediction. For example, some children report that their thought in a given situation is, "I will be scared/nervous." If such a response is given, the child should be asked about the bad result they expect to happen. In other words, "*Why* will you be scared/nervous?" The reason to avoid stating emotions as the feared outcome is that they are not inevitable, but depend on the individual's own action—that is, on how well they use the realistic thinking. This makes the whole process rather confused. For example, if a child about to give a talk were to think, "I will get embarrassed," how realistic this is depends on how good she is at thinking realistically. In contrast, beliefs focusing on somatic symptoms of anxiety, such as "I will go red" or "I will tremble," are suitable to work with. Thoughts centering on physiological aspects of anxiety are often relevant to social fears and are very amenable to examining evidence. So, in brief, step 1 involves identifying a clear and specific statement of the negative prediction in a situation, termed the "worried thought."

Step 2: Looking for Evidence for the Thought

The next step involves searching for evidence related to the unrealistic or worried thought. As the therapist, you can introduce this step by suggesting that a good way to handle worried thoughts is to have a look at what evidence there is for them. A child in an anxiety-provoking situation typically believes that there is a high probability that the negative prediction they have identified will happen. For example, a child with separation anxiety whose mother is late picking him up from school, may hold the following belief: "She has had a very serious accident." If the child believes that there is a very high probability that his mother has been in a serious accident, then he will obviously be highly anxious. If this estimate could be reduced, he would also feel less anxious. So, one of the primary aims of cognitive restructuring is to help children reduce their estimate of the probability with which they expect negative events to occur. Reducing the expected probability of negative events is often a gradual process. It is critical that people be able to truly believe the lower estimate. Even a small—but believed—reduction in the expected probability of events is better than a very low figure that a person doesn't really believe. As more evidence is gathered, the expected probability should continue to decrease over time, until the person is truly able to believe that the chances of the feared event occurring are in fact very small. This is particularly true of adults, because adults usually have very entrenched beliefs, established over many years, that may be relatively difficult to shift. Adults will often question evidence raised by the therapist and may be quite skeptical regarding new evidence. As a result, change is often in small steps. In contrast, children are often very open to challenges to their assumptions. Younger children, especially, tend to be more open to new information and often accept the therapist's suggestions almost unquestioningly.

When searching for evidence for worried thoughts, we have found the analogy of being like a detective to be very effective with children. We generally encourage younger children to nominate their favorite detective or superhero to help them look for evidence for their worried thoughts. The central point that children need to grasp is that they need to search for evidence or clues in the real world, just like a detective does, in order to decide whether their worried thoughts are really true or not. Rather than being considered as facts, identified thoughts should be seen as *ideas* that need to be tested or checked out. Useful questions for young people when searching for evidence for a worried thought include: "How do I know that this bad thing will actually happen?" and "What evidence is there that this will or will not happen?"

There are many different sources of evidence that are helpful in evaluating worried thoughts. To some extent, the nature of the belief being examined will determine the evidence that is most relevant. In the initial stages of cognitive restructuring, children should be positively reinforced with plenty of praise and attention, even for suggesting vaguely relevant evidence. Some of the commonly used sources of evidence include: (a) past experience, (b) alternative possibilities, (c) general knowledge, and (d) taking a different perspective.

Past Experience

This is one of the simplest forms of evidence for children to identify. Usually, there have been many prior occasions when the child expected a negative outcome in a situation but the actual outcome was far more pleasant. So, thinking back to what has happened before is often a valuable piece of evidence. In the case of the child who holds the belief that her mother has had a very serious accident, a useful question might be, "Has your Mom ever had a serious accident before?" Hopefully, the answer will be no. (If she has, then how often becomes a crucial point.) This type of information often produces ideal evidence. So, a simple question children can be taught to ask themselves during the anxiety-provoking situation is: "What has happened before in this situation?"

When asking about previous experiences, you may sometimes come across people (particularly adolescents with more severe symptoms) who repeatedly report negative outcomes in nearly all of the past events they recall. Such individuals may find it very difficult to recall *any* positive aspects of a situation that would serve as useful evidence against their negative beliefs. One way to address this difficulty is to teach young people to focus their attention on the actual details of the situation rather than on their feelings or perceptions of events. For example, a child who says that he remembers making a complete fool of himself during the last school play should be asked details about exactly what happened. Did he forget all his lines, half his lines … a quarter … or maybe only one or two? Is anyone really likely to remember? The idea of being a complete fool is an interpretation. When the situation is looked at objectively, it may become clear that the situation was not nearly as bad as it seems. In addition, children who recall bad experiences (perhaps real) may need to gather some new evidence for themselves. The technique of prediction testing, discussed later in this chapter, is an ideal method for producing such evidence.

Alternative Possibilities

Another form of evidence that is easy for children to access is the alternative possibility to the negative prediction. Anxious children often narrowly focus on the negative event they expect to occur without considering the other possible outcomes. In the case of the child who holds the belief that her mother has had a very serious accident, the child may be fixed on the idea that that is the *only* reason her mother is late. Typically, other plausible explanations, such as "She has been held up in traffic" or "She got caught up doing the shopping," are not considered. The child interprets her mother's lateness as definite evidence that her mother has been harmed.

Asking children to generate other alternative outcomes is a highly effective way of reducing the expected probability of the negative event because it shifts the focus off the negative prediction and onto other possibilities. Accepting the fact that there are several possible outcomes in a given situation is incongruent with the belief that the feared event will definitely occur. Therefore, as the alternative possibilities are considered, the probability of the threatening event usually decreases. The desired goal is for the child to eventually come to the conclusion that the probability of the feared event occurring is actually quite small, and it is more likely that the outcome is far less threatening than was predicted. Introducing less threatening possibilities helps children begin to think more realistically about the anxiety-provoking situations that they face. Useful questions that help children generate alternative outcomes include, "What else could happen?" or "What other possibilities are there?"

General Knowledge

Searching for relevant facts, figures, and information about the negative prediction can also provide useful evidence. For example, relevant information regarding the belief "My mother is late because she has been in a dangerous accident" could include asking the child how many of her friends have been involved in car accidents and how many of those actually suffered serious injuries. The idea is to reduce the estimated probability of the negative event by getting the child to put her expectation into a broader context. For example, "So, of all of your friends and relatives, you can only think of one person who had a bad car accident and that was three years ago. Is it really very likely, then, that your mother has had one now?"

Another effective technique for gathering this form of evidence is to encourage children to go into the anxiety-provoking situation and observe particular features in vivo. For example, one child believed that others were continually watching him and thinking bad things about him as he walked down the street. For homework, he was asked to walk down the street and count the number of people who were actually looking at him. He found that the number of people who looked at him was very small and that there was very little evidence to suggest they were evaluating him in a negative manner. In a similar fashion, children can sometimes be given practice exercises that require them to look up certain facts or figures using libraries or the Internet. For example, a child who lives in a safe area but worries every night that he will be hurt by a burglar could be asked to look up burglary rates in his area and then find out how many homes are in his area. He can then calculate his real chances of being such a victim.

Taking a Different Perspective

Finally, children can gather valuable evidence by learning to look at situations from another person's perspective. For example, it was helpful for the child in the previous example to imagine that *he* was standing in the street watching another boy walk past, and to think about whether he would be thinking negative things about that boy. He reported that he wouldn't evaluate people walking by in a negative manner, and was able to use this as evidence to suggest that other people would also be unlikely to evaluate him negatively. This technique for gathering evidence typically works best with adolescents, particularly those with social fears, and may be more difficult for younger children to grasp.

The primary aim of step 2 is to teach children how to find useful evidence, in any way they can, about their worried thoughts. We have found that the evidence that is most frequently used by children is past experience and alternative possibilities. Older adolescents and adults, especially those with social fears, do well with taking a different perspective. Reminding younger children to think about how their detective figure might see the situation is a very good strategy.

Step 3: Evaluating the Thought on the Basis of the Evidence

The next step is to evaluate the thought on the basis of the evidence gathered. In essence, the question to be answered here is, "Having looked at all the evidence, how likely is it really that the negative event I am worried about will occur?" Children need to be taught how to look at all the evidence they have generated, and decide upon a realistic estimate based on that evidence. A useful question for children to ask themselves at this point is, "Based on the evidence, how likely is it that the bad thing I'm expecting will actually happen?" Hopefully, the estimate will be reduced, and the end result will be a more realistic way of thinking. The desired goal is to reduce the estimate of the negative prediction, thereby reducing anxiety. Some adolescents and parents may be able to work well with probabilities—for example, a 10 percent chance, 5 percent chance, and so on, whereas others will find percentages conceptually difficult. Those who don't like percentages may find it easier to work with qualitative labels, such as "very likely," "moderately likely," and "not very likely." For younger children, it is probably best to ignore the concept of probabilities and simply contrast different ways of thinking in the form of "worried thinking" and "calm thinking." The crucial point to make about most anxiety-provoking situations is that they usually turn out to be not nearly as bad as we had expected them to be.

We have found that the best way for children to learn the technique of gathering evidence and evaluating worried thoughts is by working through many examples in the sessions. Children usually benefit from seeing the examples written down, either on a dry-erase board or a large sheet of paper. Groups are especially useful here because the children can all brainstorm evidence and help each other, but the technique also works well in individual therapy. Parents should be taken through a similar process, with examples that are relevant to their own situation.

Step 4: Examining the Consequences of the Feared Event

A final step that can often be useful for some adolescents and adults involves challenging the consequences of the feared outcome. This step is best introduced after the basic concepts of cognitive restructuring have been grasped. We have found this technique to be most appropriate with adolescents and more mature children (as well as parents), as it can be difficult for younger children to grasp. The step involves learning how to identify and challenge the consequences believed to be connected with the feared event. The aim is to address the typical overestimation of the cost of the negative event. Simple questions that can help identify the catastrophic consequences include, "What is the worst that could happen here?" or "What is the worst-case scenario if the thing I'm worried about really does occur?" The answer will usually be the expected negative consequence.

Once the feared consequence has been identified, it can be treated as yet another negative prediction and challenged using evidence, as previously outlined. The important concept to convey here is that even if the worst does happen, it usually isn't as bad as we think it will be, and we can always work out ways to handle it. Helpful questions young people can ask themselves are, "Is the worst that could happen really so bad?" and "How could I handle it if the worst did happen?" Formulating possible coping strategies helps create a sense of control and mastery, resulting in a decrease in anxiety.

Practice

At the end of the sessions on cognitive restructuring, children and parents should have an understanding of (a) the link between thoughts and feelings, (b) the types of thoughts that lead to feelings of anxiety, and (c) how to use evidence to change these thoughts and reduce anxiety. From this point, regular and consistent practice of realistic thinking is critical. Children will need to work hard at challenging worried thoughts both in and out of sessions. Many examples will need to be worked through in order to produce substantial changes in unhelpful patterns of thinking.

The importance of practice and positive reinforcement needs to be emphasized to parents. Parental involvement will be particularly necessary with younger children. Positive reinforcement, in the form of praise, rewards, and attention, following the completion of practice tasks will be crucial for both younger children and adolescents. Parents should also get into the habit of asking their children "challenge" questions whenever they express worries or fears. These questions should be aimed at reminding the child to examine evidence: "What is it you are worried about?" "Has that ever happened before?" "Are there any other ways of looking at it?" Parents should begin to use these prompting questions as a way of reminding the child to think more realistically rather than simply providing reassurance and advice. Eventually, a simple prompt such as, "Why don't you try your detective thinking?" will be enough. Of course, parents should also be encouraged to practice realistic thinking for their own fears and worries. Those parents who don't experience (or don't admit to) anxiety can be encouraged to practice the strategies in response to stress or even anger, simply for the purpose of improving their comfort with the technique so that they can better help their child.

Sample exercises 4 and 5 involve recording evidence and evaluating worried thoughts. In exercise 4, Detective Thinking, children record the anxiety-provoking event, the negative prediction, the evidence gathered, and a "calm thought" to reflect another, less anxiety-provoking alternative possibility.

Sample exercise 5, Realistic Thinking, should only be used with older children, adolescents, and parents, because it reflects step 4, in which the consequences of the feared event are examined. In the last part of this exercise, children record the worst outcome they believe could occur, and ways they

Detective Thinking

Event _____

What am I worried about?	
What is the evidence? What happened when I was worried before? What are the facts? What else could happen?	
What is my calm thought? What will really happen?	

Event _____

What am I worried about?	
What is the evidence? What happened when I was worried before? What are the facts? What else could happen?	
What is my calm thought? What will really happen?	

Sample Exercise 4

Realistic Thinking

Event _____

What am I worried about?	
What is the evidence? What happened when I was worried before? What are the facts? What else could happen?	
What is my calm thought? What will really happen?	
So what if it does happen?	

Event _____

What am I worried about?	
What is the evidence? What happened when I was worried before? What are the facts? What else could happen?	
What is my calm thought? What will really happen?	
So what if it does happen?	

Sample Exercise 5

could handle it. This exercise is generally best introduced after young people are familiar with the basic techniques and principles of cognitive restructuring and are confident in completing exercise 4. The exercises should be reviewed during each session, and appropriate feedback should be given. If time permits, it is often useful to devote more than one session completely to cognitive restructuring, because it is a technique that many clients find difficult at first. Examples from the week should be discussed in detail. Several subsequent sessions should continue to devote at least some time to discussing cognitive restructuring homework and correcting difficulties. Remember that children will require plenty of praise and rewards for their efforts at practice.

Case Study Examples

Sally

(Sally is the seven-year-old girl with a principal diagnosis of separation anxiety disorder and an additional diagnosis of specific phobia, animal type. See chapter 3 for a more thorough review of Sally's background.)

Therapist: When you first came to see me, Sally, I remember that you told me that you were scared of dogs. I was wondering, could you think back to the last time you were near a dog?

Sally: Yes, a few weeks ago I saw a dog in the street.

Therapist: Could you tell me a bit about it?

Sally: Well, I was going for a walk down our street with my sister, and this big black dog came out from its kennel.

Therapist: What happened then?

Sally: It started walking toward us as we walked past.

Therapist: How did you feel when it started coming toward you?

Sally   I was really scared.

Therapist: I can understand that you would have felt scared. Can you remember what you were thinking would happen?

Sally: I was thinking that the dog was going to bite me.

Therapist: So your worried thought was, "The dog is going to bite me." What could you have done to cope?

Sally: I could have run away from the dog.

Therapist: I guess that is one thing you could have done, although it is usually better to just stand still when a dog is coming up to you. What could you have done to change your worried thought, that the dog would bite you?

Sally: I could have thought about something else.

Therapist: Good idea. Let's talk a bit about what you could have thought about instead. Changing your worried thought is a good step toward feeling less scared. We need to look at the evidence for your worried thought about the dog. Have there been any other times when a dog came up to you?

Sally: I suppose so.

Therapist: Tell me about what happened at those times. Did the dog bite you?

Sally: No it didn't bite me. It came up to me and sniffed me.

Therapist: Good. So at other times when a dog has come up to you, it didn't bite you. Instead of the dog biting you, what else could have happened?

Sally: I don't know.

Therapist: Well, what else might it be doing when it comes up to you?

Sally: Maybe it just wants to sniff me.

Therapist: Good! So it is possible that the dog might be mean, but it is also possible that the dog might be friendly. Was the black dog you saw when you were with your sister friendly?

Sally: Yes. My sister patted it, but I didn't want to.

Therapist: Okay, that's another useful piece of evidence. Now that we have looked at some evidence, do you think your worried thought that the dog was going to bite you was really likely?

Sally: Probably not.

Therapist: Good work. From the evidence we came up with it is probably more likely that it was friendly and that nothing bad would happen.

Sally: Yes.

Therapist: I'm wondering, how would you be feeling if you were thinking that the dog was going to bite you?

Sally: Scared.

Therapist: And how would you be feeling if you were thinking that the dog was friendly?

Sally: Good.

Therapist: Excellent. So you can see that your worried thinking about the dog would make you feel scared, and these other calm thoughts would make you feel more happy and relaxed around the dog.

Sally's Detective Thinking

Event   *A big dog came toward me*

What am I worried about?	*The dog is going to bite me.*
What is the evidence? What happened when I was worried before? What are the facts? What else could happen?	*Other dogs have come upto me before, and they didn't bite me.* *The other possibility is that the dog is friendly and wants me to pat him.*
What is my calm thought? What will really happen?	*The dog might really just want to play with me.*

Table 7: Sally's Detective Thinking

Jessica

(Twelve-year-old Jessica meets criteria for a principal diagnosis of generalized anxiety disorder and an additional diagnosis of specific phobia, blood-injury type. See chapter 3 for a more thorough review of Jessica's background.)

Therapist: I was wondering if you could tell me how things have been this week, Jessica.

Jessica: Not too bad.

Therapist: How has school been?

Jessica: Terrible. The teachers have been giving us so much homework to do.

Therapist: How has the homework been going?

Jessica: Basically it hasn't. I hate it. It takes me so long, and it's hard.

Therapist: It sounds like you might be feeling quite anxious about the homework.

Jessica:	Yes, I get a sick feeling in my stomach when I have to face it, and I keep putting it off as long as possible.
Therapist:	It is understandable that you would be putting it off if you are feeling so anxious about it. Can you work out what you are worried will happen if you do your homework?
Jessica:	I guess I'm worried that I will make mistakes.
Therapist:	I see. What do you think would happen if you did make mistakes in your homework?
Jessica:	I would get into trouble.
Therapist:	Good. So maybe your worried thought is something like, "I will make mistakes in my homework and get into trouble." Does this sound about right?
Jessica:	Yes, I think so.
Therapist:	When you say that you might get into trouble, what exactly do you mean? Do you mean that you will get detention or have to stay back after class?
Jessica:	No, I mean that the teacher will scream at me.
Therapist:	I see, so you are worried that you will make mistakes on your homework and that the teacher will scream at you in class. Let's look at the evidence for this thought. How can you be sure that the teacher will scream at you if you make mistakes on your homework?
Jessica:	I don't know.
Therapist:	Well, for example, have other people made mistakes on their homework?
Jessica:	Yes, lots of people make mistakes.
Therapist:	Has the teacher ever yelled at other people in the class for making mistakes on their homework?
Jessica:	Not really.
Therapist:	So other people have made mistakes on their homework, and she hasn't screamed at them. That sounds like a good piece of evidence to me. I was wondering whether you have ever made mistakes before on your homework?
Jessica:	Yes, of course.
Therapist:	What happened on those occasions, did your teacher yell at you?
Jessica:	No, she didn't.
Therapist:	What did she actually do?

Jessica: Nothing. She didn't say anything.

Therapist: So at this point we don't have much reason to believe that if you make mistakes on your homework, which everyone does, that she will scream at you. You might remember that one type of evidence we talked about was the alternative possibility. Rather than your teacher screaming at you for making mistakes on your homework, what might be an alternative possibility, Jessica?

Jessica: That she doesn't say anything.

Therapist: Excellent. So it is possible that she might yell at you, but it is also possible that she might not say anything. What about the possibility that she might help you understand the mistakes you made, so that you can become even cleverer than you already are?

Jessica: Yes, that's a possibility.

Therapist: Okay, so when you first arrived at the session, you thought that it was very likely that if you made mistakes on your homework, your teacher would yell at you. Now that we have looked at the evidence, we can see that there are at least two other possibilities—that she doesn't say anything, or that she helps you so that you can improve. Now how likely do you think it is that your teacher will scream at you for making mistakes on your homework—very likely, moderately likely, or not very likely?

Jessica: I think, not very likely.

Therapist: So then, what else might happen?

Jessica: I guess she would just tell me to do better next time.

This is a good start in challenging Jessica's worries about homework. The next obvious step would involve challenging the consequences of the belief, as discussed in step 4, earlier in this chapter. In other words, so what if the teacher screams at you? Hopefully, over time Jessica should be able to realize that even if her teacher did yell at her, although it would be unpleasant, it would pass with no further consequences. However, children first need to become confident in identifying and challenging worried thoughts before they are ready to not be too affected if the worst does happen.

Simon

(Simon is a fifteen-year-old who meets criteria for a principal diagnosis of social phobia and an additional diagnosis of major depressive disorder. See chapter 3 for a more thorough review of Simon's background.)

The initial part of this discussion with Simon focused on his social anxiety about asking a girl out on a date. His main worry was that he would make many mistakes and stutter very badly. After looking at the evidence for this worry, he quickly realized that the probability of it occurring was in fact quite low. Having looked at the probability of the negative event, the next step in the session is to challenge the consequences of the negative event. One way this could be done is as follows.

Therapist: Okay, so when you first came to the session you thought that it was very likely that you would make many mistakes and stutter if you asked Christina out on a date. Now that we have looked at the evidence, it seems that the more likely scenario is that you will be able to talk to her without stuttering and mixing up your words. Even so, I am interested to know what you think would happen if you did stutter severely and mix up your words.

Simon: That would be awful—I would be totally humiliated, and she would reject me.

Therapist: Can you tell me exactly what you mean when you say that Christina would "reject" you?

Simon: Well, she would think that I was a total idiot and would refuse to go out on a date with me. In fact, I suspect that she would never speak to me again.

Therapist: Now that we've worked out what you are worried will happen, it could be helpful to look at the evidence for this thought. What evidence is there that she would think you were a total idiot and never speak to you again, because you mixed up some words and stuttered?

Simon: I don't know. She is really together, and I suppose she would look down on someone like me.

Therapist: I want you to imagine that you are very together. Every word you pronounce is perfect, and you have excellent social skills. Now imagine that you are at a party, and someone else comes up to you and tries to make conversation. Even though they are doing their best, they make lots of mistakes and stutter. What would you think of them?

Simon: I would think that they had guts for coming up and starting a conversation, even though they were obviously nervous.

Therapist: That's interesting. So you wouldn't think that they were a complete idiot for making mistakes and stuttering?

Simon: No, probably not.

Therapist: Let's go back to asking Christina out. One possibility is that she might think that you are a fool. What are some other possibilities?

Simon: She could feel sorry for me.

Simon's Realistic Thinking

Event ___*Asking a girl out on a date*___

What am I worried about?	*I am going to mix up my words/stutter, and she will totally reject me.*
What is the evidence? What happened when I was worried before? What are the facts? What else could happen?	*I have had success asking a girl out on a date before.* *She might not think I am an idiot and reject me. She could even be flattered that I asked her out.*
What is my calm thought? What will really happen?	*It should be okay. I probably won't stutter or be totally rejected.*
So what if it does happen?	*Even if the worst does happen, I could cope with it by talking about it to my best mate.* *It would not really affect my life that much, and in time I would get over it.* *Lots of other people like me. Ultimately, it doesn't really matter if she doesn't.*

Table 8: Simon's Realistic Thinking

Therapist: That's one possibility. What else could happen?

Simon: There's a chance that she could be flattered that I asked her out, even if I did do a bad job of it.

Therapist: That could be. Have you ever asked a girl out on a date before?

Simon: I asked a girl out for a milkshake about a year ago.

Therapist: How did it go?

Simon: Not too bad. She agreed to go and we had a good time.

Therapist:	So in summary, you have had success asking a girl out before, and even though one possibility is that she will reject you, there are several other possibilities, including that she will be flattered. Now how likely do you think it is that she will reject you, even if you did stutter?
Simon:	Not very likely.
Therapist:	Good. Now that we have looked at the probability of this outcome, I want you to squarely face it. Even if the worst does happen, and she rejects you, how bad would this really be?
Simon:	Well, it would be pretty awful.
Therapist:	Yes, it would be pretty awful, but does it really matter if she thinks poorly of you?
Simon:	I don't know. It would be bad for a while.
Therapist:	How long do you think she would think poorly of you?
Simon:	I guess until she forgets about it.
Therapist:	Could you make a guess of how long this might be?
Simon:	Probably only a couple of weeks.
Therapist:	How would this affect your life?
Simon:	Not very much when I think about it like that. I suppose other people would still like me even if she didn't.
Therapist:	Do you think that you could get over it?
Simon:	In time I could.
Therapist:	What could you do to cope?
Simon:	I could talk to my friend Andrew about it, or distract myself.
Therapist:	Good ideas, Simon. If this happened, you could also try thinking about the reasons why she acted the way she did. It might be something more to do with her than with you.

Prediction Testing

One additional technique—prediction testing—is worthy of mention, particularly in the treatment of generalized anxiety disorder. Prediction testing involves challenging a negative prediction by testing it out in vivo, and gathering real-life evidence in the process. The anxious individual attempts to find out whether his prediction comes true, and in doing so builds up a body of useful evidence. Prediction testing is particularly effective with younger children who may have difficulty spontaneously generating evidence, or with chronic worriers who show highly rigid patterns of unrealistic thinking.

Prediction testing is perhaps best illustrated with an example. Let's consider Jessica, who, in addition to worrying about her homework, is also chronically worried about being late to school. Prediction testing would involve setting up a scenario in which Jessica is intentionally late in order to test out what happens. If her worried thought is "I will get into big trouble," the purpose of prediction testing would be to see whether this prediction in fact comes true. Usually the outcome is not as bad as the prediction, which provides valuable evidence against the worried thought. This technique is really the precursor to in vivo exposure, which is dealt with in detail in chapter 8.

Dealing with Difficulties

Difficulty Grasping Concepts

Some children may show difficulties grasping the rationale and technique of cognitive restructuring. In the face of difficulties, the importance of consistent, repeated practice cannot be emphasized enough. Unrealistic patterns of thinking are typically highly automatic, habitual, and may be out of conscious awareness, so considerable time and effort to shift worried thoughts may be needed. In addition, cognitive restructuring, like any new skill, will initially seem difficult and unfamiliar to most children. During the course of the program, children will need to work through many examples, both in and out of session, in order to master the techniques. As a first step, children who are struggling should be encouraged to practice regularly, with guidance from both parents and therapists. A review of the material covered in the session is usually helpful, and the child should be allowed to work at her own pace as much as possible. For example, a child may need to spend several sessions working on the link between thoughts and feelings before she is ready to move on to the steps involved in challenging worried thoughts. Prediction testing, as previously noted, is an excellent strategy for targeting more rigid patterns of thinking, particularly in cases of generalized anxiety.

Inability to Comprehend

In some cases a child may genuinely lack the cognitive ability or concentration to understand the principles of cognitive restructuring in this format. In this case an alternative form of cognitive restructuring known as "self-instructional training" (Meichenbaum 1977) may be more suitable. Self-instructional training has been shown to be particularly useful for very young children and those with intellectual/learning difficulties or attention deficit hyperactivity disorder. In essence, self-instructional training involves teaching children to replace threatening self-talk with coping statements. Children are not required to look for evidence for worried thoughts, but simply to replace them with calm ones. In brief, self-instructional training involves the following steps: (a) the child is taught to identify the worried thoughts, (b) the therapist models appropriate self-statements that stress personal adequacy, counteract worry, and reinforce successful performance, (c) the child then practices saying the calm self-statements to himself out loud and the therapist provides feedback, and (d) the child practices repeating the self-statements covertly, in real-life situations. Ultimately, if neither form of cognitive restructuring is effective, it may be best to leave it and focus on other strategies, especially exposure (chapter 8). For some children, relaxation (the subject of the next chapter) may be a better anxiety-management strategy than cognitive restructuring.

Overwhelmed by Emotion

Some children may be able to competently describe the principles of cognitive restructuring in session and even do well with role plays, but may report considerable difficulty using the technique in real-life settings because they become paralyzed with anxiety. In these cases, we have found the use of cue cards to be effective. Critical questions that children can ask themselves during the various steps (such as, "What am I worried will happen here?") are written on small cards. In the anxiety-provoking situation, the child pulls out these cards to remind herself of the steps she needs to go through to challenge thoughts. For example, one young girl feared that if her mother left the house to go shopping, she would never return. When her mother did go out, the girl became so anxious that she couldn't remember her detective thinking. A useful cue for her was, "What usually happens when your mother goes out?" Reading this question on the card cued her to remember that "Mom always comes back," and her distress on separation was gradually reduced with repeated cognitive challenging and exposure.

Chapter 6

Relaxation

Various relaxation techniques have been developed for use with adults, including progressive muscle relaxation, guided imagery, autogenic training, and meditation. Techniques for children and adolescents have generally followed similar lines. In particular, muscle relaxation techniques have been shown to be effective in the treatment of anxiety for both adults (Borkovec and Costello 1993) and children (Eisen and Silverman 1993), with results maintained for at least six months. Research has generally failed to demonstrate any major differences between techniques in efficacy or effects, so which technique you and your client choose is a matter of personal preference. The technique that we prefer for children includes a combination of muscle tension and relaxation, together with the use of relaxing images and thoughts. Relaxation techniques for children should be developmentally sensitive: exercises need to be kept simple and short to accommodate limits in concentration and attention, and clear, step-by-step demonstrations, with frequent repetition and regular monitoring by the therapist, is essential during sessions. In addition, instructions should be sensitive to children's developing cognitive and language abilities. As the therapist, you can achieve this best by using simple language and avoiding excessive verbal information. As with other aspects of anxiety management for children, parental involvement and monitoring is vital.

The approach outlined in this book is a brief form of progressive muscle relaxation based loosely on the procedures outlined by Bernstein and Borkovec (1973). This technique involves tensing, then relaxing, individual muscle groups of the body, in addition to using relaxing imagery and self-talk. Relaxation is widely used to target the somatic symptoms of anxiety, but it is also helpful for the cognitive aspects of anxiety. The exact mechanisms by which it works are unclear.

In our experience, relaxation training may not be necessary for all anxious children and adolescents. Research at our clinic involving a program that does not include a relaxation-training component demonstrated significant reductions in anxiety symptoms. We conclude that cognitive restructuring and exposure appear to be sufficient to produce substantial reductions in anxiety for most children. We introduce relaxation here as an additional technique that may be of value in some cases, either in addition to or in place of cognitive restructuring. Relaxation may be especially relevant in cases where children have a great deal of difficulty using cognitive strategies, perhaps for intellectual or developmental reasons. In addition, in cases where concentration and ability to sit still are low, relaxation may provide an important avenue to try and develop these skills. Parents' preferences are obviously important; it is not worth attempting relaxation if motivation to practice is low.

Relaxation training is best introduced in treatment by outlining the rationale and benefits of this technique. To begin, children need to develop an awareness of how they feel when they are tense versus how they feel when they are relaxed. After this understanding is reached, you should lead children through the relaxation exercise during the session. The relaxation exercises are kept relatively short, around fifteen minutes (although in some cases it may be necessary to decrease to as few as five minutes in the early stages), because younger children typically have a limited attention span. At the end of the first practice, children should be able to start doing relaxation at home. For younger children, we usually recommend that parents learn relaxation together with the child in session so that home-practice sessions can be conducted together. In fact, it is often a good idea to encourage the parents to introduce a regular relaxation session for the entire family or at least to join their child for relaxation practice themselves. You should continue to conduct relaxation sessions with the child and the parents, if appropriate, for the following three to four sessions to allow any difficulties to be addressed. Between sessions, children should be practicing at home on a daily basis. Relaxation practice should be reviewed during sessions, where progress can be monitored and problems addressed.

Introducing Relaxation to Children

Step 1: Explaining the Purpose and Benefits of Relaxation

Children and parents both profit from an understanding of the purpose and benefits of relaxation. To begin with, both will be more likely to put effort into practice if they understand how it may help them be less anxious. Therefore, the main benefits of relaxation need to be outlined.

Relaxation techniques will help you:

- feel calm and relaxed

- feel more in control

- have less tension in your body

- be less nervous

- have better concentration

- enjoy a more peaceful sleep

- have fewer stomachaches and headaches

- be able to enjoy things more

Step 2: Tension versus Relaxation

Initially, children need to develop an awareness of the difference between being tense and being relaxed. To begin, you should remind the child of the discussion from the previous session regarding the changes that occur in their bodies when they feel nervous or worried.

The next step is to contrast the state of being anxious with that of being relaxed, so children can differentiate between them. You might begin by saying, "I want you think back to a time when you felt happy and calm. What was the situation you were in? How did it feel to be calm and relaxed? What was your body like when you were relaxed? What sorts of things were you thinking about? How is this different from when you are feeling worried?" Brainstorm the features of a relaxed body, such as a calm heart, a still body, and loose muscles, and contrast these with the features of a tense body. A useful exercise is to ask children to tense some part of their body, such as their hand, and then to let it relax. Contrast the feelings in each state. Similarly, you can ask children to think about something that worries them, and then about something fun or pleasant. Again contrast the experience in each state. A helpful exercise for use with groups is to ask children to pretend to be relaxed or tense, and have other group members guess their state by looking at their body and facial expression. Younger children can pretend that they are a stiff robot, and then a rag doll, a jellyfish, or a loose rubber band. Ask them how it felt to be very stiff and tense, and then how it felt to be calm and relaxed. Useful words to describe feeling relaxed are "calm," "floppy," and "still." The main points you need to make are:

1. When we get worried or nervous, many changes happen in our body and mind.

2. These changes are normal and happen to everyone.

3. Learning to recognize these changes and know when you're feeling scared is the first step toward coping with anxiety.

4. Being calm and relaxed feels very different from being tense.

Introducing Relaxation to Parents

In a group setting, it is probably easier to run the parent session separately from the children due to the sheer size of the group. In individual therapy, parents may be included with their child to learn relaxation or they could be taught separately if the child prefers them not to be there (this is true for many adolescents). The same concepts presented to children need to be briefly covered with parents: you need to provide information on the general changes associated with anxiety that may be reduced through relaxation, and the purpose and benefits of relaxation. Parents need a detailed, step-by-step understanding of the relaxation exercise, so it's useful to lead a short relaxation exercise with parents during the session, assuming they have not been included in their child's practice. Parents who are themselves anxious should be encouraged to practice relaxation for their own benefit as well. You might point out that relaxation is a skill that is learned, and improves with practice. Parents should be aware of the need to encourage and assist their children in implementing regular practice. Remind them that rewards and praise are powerful reinforcements for practice.

Distractions

Several conditions in the environment can be arranged to assist in minimizing distractions and helping children focus attention during relaxation training. Minimizing distractions during relaxation is necessary in the initial stages of relaxation training, but once children have mastered relaxation skills, they should be encouraged to try out their skills in more distracting or stressful situations.

Initially, it is important to find a quiet room that is neither too cold nor too warm. It may be helpful to dim the lights, if possible. The child can either sit in a chair or lie on the floor. He needs to position himself comfortably, with good posture, and with all his limbs resting freely. Any tight clothing should be loosened. The child should be asked to close his eyes. Sometimes children become nervous about not being allowed to move during relaxation, so you may want to explain that it is okay for them to shift the position of their body during the session if they start to feel uncomfortable. Similarly, some children find it frightening to close their eyes. If this occurs, reassure the child that he may leave his eyes open, and suggest that he focus on a certain point in the room, such as a spot on the floor.

Guiding Your Client through Relaxation

During the relaxation session, try to talk slowly and make your voice sound gentle and calm. Your tone of voice should mirror the tension-and-release components of the exercise. Your voice should have an almost hypnotic quality to it, with pauses between instructions to give the child time to carry them out. As you give the instructions, monitor the child so that you can give assistance if you notice that she is experiencing difficulties. Actually doing the tensing and relaxing with the client can help make your timing more realistic.

Adults in relaxation training will typically work with a large number of muscle groups, but with children it is important to work with just a small number, in order to keep the relaxation short and simple. For younger children, focus on around three or four muscle groups, such as arms and hands, head and face, and stomach and legs. For adolescents, the various muscle groups can be broken down further.

The main steps of relaxation are tensing the muscle, isolating the muscle, concentrating on the feelings, and relaxing the muscle. At the same time, the focus of attention is directed toward the sensations within the body and toward calming images and thoughts. The child is encouraged to say the word "relax" to herself as she releases the muscle, and to visualize the tension leaving her body.

1. **Tense** The first step in deep muscle relaxation involves tensing the specific muscle group. By doing this, the child will learn what her muscles feel like when they are tense. The child needs to tense to the point that the muscles feel stiff and tight, but not so much that it hurts. Repeating the imagery of a robot is a good idea with younger children. Explain to them that being able to identify when they feel anxious is the first step in dealing with anxiety.

2. **Isolate** The child needs to try to isolate the tension in the muscle group being worked on as much as possible. The idea is that the other muscle groups of the body remain as relaxed as possible. Throughout the process, you need to remind the child to mentally check the rest of her body to make sure that the other muscles are relaxed. At first children may have difficulty with this, but they usually become more competent with practice. This may not be a necessary component for younger children who may find it particularly difficult to master.

3. **Concentrate** While working on a particular muscle group, the tension should be held for around five seconds. During this time, the child needs to be directed to concentrate on the feeling in her muscles. Remind her of the words she previously came up with to describe a tense body.

4. **Relax** After the five seconds of tension, the child should relax the muscles quickly. The aim is to let the muscles completely flop, releasing all traces of tension. At this point it is helpful for children to focus on the relaxed feeling in the muscles, and to continue to let go of any remaining tension. Again, remind the child of the words (floppy, calm, heavy) and images (rag doll, jellyfish) they used earlier to describe a relaxed body. Ask children to say the word "relax" to themselves as they release the tension in their muscles. Describe the drifting away of worries and tension with phrases such as "a cloud drifting across the sky" or "a leaf floating down a river."

A Sample Script

A detailed script for the relaxation exercise is provided below. With appropriate pauses, it should take around fifteen minutes. However, plenty of time should be allowed for the first relaxation session , because children may experience difficulty their first time. (See the Dealing with Difficulties section at the end of the chapter for more information.)

This exercise focuses on four muscle groups: arms, face, stomach, and legs. If the child is very young and/or fidgety, you may need to break the script into two segments, separated by a break.

"I'd like you to sit on a chair, or lie on the floor, so that you feel comfortable. Let all the parts of your body rest on the chair or the floor. I am going to teach you a relaxation exercise today, to help you feel calmer and more relaxed. I will go through it step by step and tell you what to do, so you just need to listen to my voice and follow the steps. I will be asking you to squeeze some of the muscles in your body really tight, and then to let them go floppy again. You will not have to do anything that you don't want to, and if you are having any problems, just let me know. Okay, I'd like you to lie back and close your eyes. Good.

"Let's start with your arms. I'd like you to stretch out your arms in front of you, so that they are really straight. Now take a deep breath, and clench your fists really tight, and squeeze all of the muscles in your arms as though you are squeezing the water out of a sponge. That's it, hold it . . . and relax. Breathe out, and let your arms flop down by your side. Notice how heavy your arms feel. Imagine that your arms are like soft pieces of spaghetti, very floppy. Quietly say the word 'relax' to yourself as you breathe out. Feel yourself becoming very calm, very relaxed. Try to let any worries go, and just think about how relaxed you feel. Enjoy feeling so calm.

"Now we'll go on to the muscles of your face. I'd like you to take a breath, and screw up the muscles of your face, really tight so that you look very wrinkly. Screw up the muscles around your eyes, your nose, and push your lips together. Don't worry if it looks funny, just notice how tight it feels. That's good . . . now hold it, hold it . . . and relax. Say the word 'relax' to yourself as you breathe out. Let all the muscles in your face go floppy, like jelly. Let your eyes go heavy and droopy, and let your lips fall apart a little. Feel yourself sinking down, feeling very heavy, very relaxed. Let all the tightness drift away, so that you become completely relaxed. Very calm.

"Let's move on to the muscles of your tummy. I want you to take a deep breath, and hold it while you pull the muscles of your stomach in almost as though it might touch your back, really tight. Hold it, one more moment, that's it . . . and relax. Breathe out, and say the word 'relax' to yourself. Let your tummy go all loose and floppy. Relax all the muscles in your tummy. Just let go, and sink deeper and deeper into the chair/floor. Notice the difference between a tight tummy and a relaxed tummy. Don't think about anything else but the heavy feeling of your body. If any other thoughts come into your head, just let them drift away like a fluffy white cloud across the blue sky. Enjoy being so calm, so relaxed.

"The last exercise is for the muscles of your legs. I'd like you to stretch out your legs, and hold them really straight as though they are the legs of a robot. Squeeze all the muscles in your legs. Squeeze the top part of your legs really tight, now the bottom part. That's good, now take a breath, and hold it tight . . . hold it . . . and relax. Breathe out, and quietly say 'relax' to yourself. Let your legs go all floppy, as if they were made of jelly. Let them get very heavy. Let your whole body go floppy, like a jellyfish or a rag doll. Just relax. Notice how good you feel being so calm, so relaxed. Let any worries or thoughts that come into your mind drift away. Notice yourself becoming more and more relaxed. Very calm.

"You've done very well. Now in a moment I am going to ask you to slowly open your eyes. Try to keep the calm, relaxed feeling as you slowly wake yourself up. Okay, let's do that now. Slowly open your eyes, and start moving each part of your body. That's it. When you are ready, slowly stand up to your feet. Good work!"

Practice

Once children have mastered the fifteen-minute relaxation exercise (which should take around two to three weeks), they can be introduced to shorter relaxation exercises. For example, you may ask them to practice simply the relaxing part of the exercise, without tensing first. Another useful exercise is to ask children to stand and tense their arms and legs at the same time for around five seconds, and then let their whole body relax. They should try to recall the relaxed feelings they have experienced during relaxation, and quietly say "relax" to themselves. It is also important for children to learn to relax in real-life situations. For several weeks they have been practicing in the quiet therapy session and in a quiet, undisturbed setting at home. But the places they will need to use relaxation as a coping strategy will not be quiet or peaceful. Therefore, an important component is to introduce applied practice. Children should be encouraged to begin to practice their shorter relaxation in settings that are not as optimal. For example, at home, practice could be done with the television on, or in the kitchen while the family goes about getting the evening meal ready. In addition, they should be encouraged to try and practice brief relaxations (without their eyes closed and with subtle tensing) in outside settings such as on the school bus, in the playground, or in the car on the way to sports practice. By this point, the child should also be engaged in exposure exercises (see chapter 8) and they should be encouraged to use brief relaxation while practicing exposure to feared situations. Ultimately, the aim is that children learn a simple strategy to help themselves relax quickly when they are faced with an anxiety-provoking situation. The benefits of being able to do this include an increased sense of control and the ability to implement other coping strategies more effectively.

Consistent and repeated practice is critical for children to master the process of relaxation. At first it is difficult for most children to relax, but over time they can become competent at relaxation, and can relax more and more quickly. Initially, children should practice relaxation for around ten to fifteen minutes every day, using the procedure introduced in the session. A relaxation-practice sheet (sample exercise 6: My Relaxation Practice) should be provided to children so they can keep a record of their relaxation practice. The four muscle groups are outlined on the sheet to remind children of the muscles they need to work on.

Remember that you need to review the family's practice each week to encourage and praise their attempts, whether successful or unsuccessful. You should continue relaxation practice in session for three to four weeks.

My Relaxation Practice

Try to practice relaxation every day for 10-15 minutes. Tense up and relax each muscle as we did in the session. The muscle groups you need to tense and relax are:

1. Arms

2. Face

3. Tummy

4. Legs

Pick a quiet place, and do your best. Good luck!
Please fill in your form every day. Circle your answer.

Did you do relaxation?			**What was your worry rating?**	
			Before	After
Monday	Yes	No	_____	_____
Tuesday	Yes	No	_____	_____
Wednesday	Yes	No	_____	_____
Thursday	Yes	No	_____	_____
Friday	Yes	No	_____	_____
Saturday	Yes	No	_____	_____
Sunday	Yes	No	_____	_____

$$\Longleftarrow \quad 0 \quad 1 \quad 2 \quad 3 \quad 4 \quad 5 \quad 6 \quad 7 \quad 8 \quad 9 \quad 10 \quad \Longrightarrow$$

Sample Exercise 6: My Relaxation Practice

A tape recording of the exercise conducted in the session can be used during practice. However, we often suggest that a parent run the session, especially for younger children. A script for parents is available in our book *Helping Your Anxious Child: A Step-by-Step Guide for Parents*. (The script for parents and the one in this book are not identical, though they are highly similar in content. Both focus on tensing and relaxing muscle groups, but the script for parents expands on the use of imagery and breathing for further relaxation.)

The important points that need to be made to children and parents about relaxation practice are:

- Regular practice is very important. Learning to relax is like learning any other new activity—it can seem difficult at first, but the more you practice the easier it will be.

- Relaxation practice should be built into the daily routine by setting aside a specified time for it.

- Parents and children need to find a quiet place where they won't be disturbed. They also need to be able to sit or lie down comfortably, though it is important not to fall asleep during practice.

- Children should fill out their relaxation practice form and bring it along to each session.

- Parents need to give children lots of positive reinforcement, in the form of praise and rewards, for completing practice. Children should also be rewarded for partial practice attempts. One powerful reinforcement for children (that may not be suitable for adolescents) is doing relaxation together as a family.

- Parents of younger children need to monitor their child's practice and assist them where necessary.

Dealing with Difficulties

Difficulty Concentrating

One of the most common problems is difficulty with concentration. The child may find that his thoughts wander, or that he is bothered by specific, intrusive worries. Or, children may find it difficult to sit still. (In fact, that is not an uncommon problem for adults, either.) Setting up quiet conditions with minimal distractions may reduce some of these problems. However, the crucial point is that concentration is a skill to be learned, and improves with practice. Concentration is like a muscle in that it becomes weak if it is not used and becomes strong with practice. Children should be taught to gently bring their attention back to the task as many times as they need to. The idea is not to get angry or upset by the thoughts, but just to let them go. As children become skilled at redirecting their attention, they should find that their thoughts wander less often. In cases where younger children are having persistent difficulties with attention, try reducing the exercises to just three to five minutes. Alternately, rich visual imagery can be incorporated into the relaxation script to make the session more interesting. For example, children could be asked to imagine that they are walking in an imaginary land, such as in a huge castle. They could tense their legs as they imagine themselves walking slowly up the stairs of the castle, tense their arms as they pull open the heavy wooden doors, and so on. If children have severe attention deficits that prevent them from responding to these suggestions, it may be best to leave relaxation and use alternative types of anxiety management until their attention improves.

Difficulty Isolating Muscles

This is another common difficulty. Find out if the child is trying to completely isolate every muscle. You may need to explain that while it is important to have some distinction between muscle groups, this can never be achieved perfectly. Muscles are connected, some more than others, and there is likely to be some transfer between groups of muscles. Beyond this, the solution is once again to encourage the child to keep practicing. Making sure that the relaxation script includes reminders to relax other muscle groups while the children are focusing on one particular group can help.

Falling Asleep

Some parents may report that their child falls asleep during relaxation practice, and they may even see this as a positive result. Children and parents need to be told that falling asleep during practice is not beneficial. Practice involves concentration and learning, and this cannot be done when you are asleep. If getting to sleep is a problem, the technique can also be used to help this difficulty. But that needs to be done at the appropriate time—at night, in bed. Practices need to be seen as a distinct session in which the aim is not to fall asleep. If the child is regularly falling asleep, you need to find out more about practice sessions. Are they being run too late? Are they being run in a soporific environment? You may suggest that practice sessions be switched to morning when the child is less tired, that the curtains remain open, that no peaceful music is played, or that the child sit up during relaxation and not lie in bed.

Chapter 7

Child Management

As discussed in previous chapters, overinvolvement and intrusiveness by the parents is an important component of the problem, in our view. This is not necessarily the parents' fault; the relationship between parent and child is most likely a reciprocal one in which an anxious and emotional child elicits increased control from a caring parent. However, where this care and control result in reduced independence and experiences for the child, they can potentially maintain anxiety. Further, not all parents are overinvolved with their anxious child and many may be engaged in very appropriate parenting. However, a fair number of parents are overinvolved and overprotective of their child and, in some cases, this can extend to quite intense and pathological levels of involvement. Further, all parents can benefit from a refresher in basic parenting strategies. For some, this will be all that is needed. For others, a central focus of therapy for the coming weeks will involve helping them gain insight into their own behaviors and helping them gradually reduce excessive control over their child.

This chapter covers five basic child-management principles: attention, independence, modeling, nonphysical punishment, and consistency. Even though parents may be familiar with these principles, it is useful to remind them of these strategies in an overt way and to help them apply these strategies to the behavior of their anxious child. The main goal is for parents to reduce control and allow their child to function in a more autonomous way.

It is also important to discuss methods that are effective in reducing and managing oppositional behaviors. Anxious children often develop behavior patterns that are difficult to manage, particularly in situations they have been eager to avoid. The parent may be faced with a child who throws tantrums, screams, cries, sulks, or becomes aggressive when faced with an anxiety-provoking situation. Breaking routines or changing the way a child faces a situation can prove very draining and difficult for parents. Helping parents deal with generally difficult behaviors will help them feel more confident about their parenting, which in turn will allow them to reduce their attempts at control.

Explaining the Principles to Parents

The basic concepts to be conveyed to parents are discussed in detail over the following pages. As you introduce these skills and outline the essential components, encourage parents to recall situations when they have used the skills successfully as well as times when these strategies may have failed. Try to work through as many examples as possible so that parents gain a good grasp of the most effective way of using the skills. If parents are having difficulties generating examples, you may want to use the examples included in this chapter. Some strategies will require more attention than others, depending on the needs of the family. You may want to demonstrate these skills in situations that are relevant to the family, perhaps by role-playing the skill. For the first practice, the parent may play the role of the child and for the second rehearsal, the roles are reversed so the parent can practice the skill. It is also important that you take any opportunity to model these skills when you are interacting with the children. For example, if the child becomes noisy while waiting for you to finish with her parent, you could take this opportunity to model clear instructions and the use of rewards to produce compliant behavior.

As their therapist, you must be mindful of the body of knowledge parents possess about their child's behavior and be respectful of cultural and religious differences that parents may have in relation to child rearing. You possess knowledge about the behavioral principles and strategies that have proved to be most effective in managing child anxiety. During treatment, your role is to allow these two knowledge stores to meet without disregarding the expertise of the parent. With this approach, therapists will enable parents to feel more confident in the management of their child's anxieties and in dealing with difficult situations as they arise. Using this approach gives the message that there is no right or wrong way of managing a child's behaviors but that certain strategies are perhaps more likely to be effective.

You'll also want to be mindful of age-appropriate information. Many strategies will change across different developmental levels. The techniques and strategies that we will discuss in this chapter are really of relevance to younger children. Adolescents, especially older ones, will require discussion of communication strategies rather than so-called parenting. Many of the same principles apply, such as listening and clear statements, but the method of delivery is obviously very different.

Attention

Attention is a powerful tool for reinforcing a child's behavior. Most children will do anything to obtain their parent's attention and approval, especially at a young age. Paying attention to a child will encourage the child's behavior, while removing attention will discourage it. Attending may be as simple as watching the child as he behaves in a way that is pleasing to the parent and withdrawing attention when it is not pleasing. Praising, rewarding, and ignoring are more specific methods of using attention to shape a child's behavior. These methods will be discussed further, but first some important issues about applying these reinforcers will be addressed.

Initially, attention can be given as a continuous reinforcement—that is, whenever the parent notices the child facing a situation that would normally cause him anxiety. However, once the child has tackled a particular task or has reached the desired target, reinforcement can become less frequent. Partial reinforcement is likely to create a more lasting effect than continual praise and reward. However, it is still important for praise to be reasonably frequent.

Reinforcement should take place immediately after the child has carried out the desired behavior. This will ensure the maximum level of effectiveness. When the parent forgets to praise the child or rewards him much later, there is a risk the child will not associate the behavior with the reinforcement.

Praise

Although instructing parents on how to praise their child may seem like a simple technique that does not need to be explicitly stated, some parents of anxious children can be resistant to giving their child praise. This is uncommon, but there are some who believe that their child does not deserve to be rewarded for doing what any other child can do. Other parents may not be so overtly opposed to praising their child but may have their own high standards or may be emotionally restricted people who are frugal with their praise. Thus, it is important to clearly outline to parents why praise is necessary and how it can be given effectively and to provide parents with feedback regarding their behavior if you see a problem.

Praising a child when she behaves courageously or appropriately can be highly effective in shaping her behavior. Praise can be given when the child completes a planned task or following an occasion where she has behaved in a way that is pleasing to the parent. However, the praise needs to be clear and specific. Encouraging a child with vague praise such as "good girl" or "well done" is far less effective than specific, clear praise such as, "Sally, you managed to stay calm and play on your own for five minutes while I went to the kitchen . . . I am very proud of you."

Encouragement not only shapes a child's behavior but can play additional roles in the child's development. Praise conveys a message to the child that she is loved and is important. Praise can help nurture her self-concept and assist her in developing a healthy opinion of herself. In addition, when parents give their children regular praise, children learn how and when to praise themselves.

In application to anxiety, the parent needs to learn to praise courageous and nonavoidant behavior. Even extremely avoidant children do certain things that require courage (for them). Parents may not even notice these behaviors in the course of their daily lives or may fail to realize the effort needed by the child to perform them. Getting the parent to brainstorm current behaviors that their child is doing but may still find slightly difficult (no matter how slight) will help raise their awareness. You can then encourage the parent to praise their child whenever they notice these behaviors.

Rewards

Parents should be encouraged to reward nonanxious or appropriate behavior. One effective reward system that is particularly useful for younger children is the star chart or use of tokens. In this method, both the parents and the child decide on a specific task. Each time the child completes the task, he receives either a star on a chart or a token. Both child and parents need to agree on both the nature of the task and the reward. Once the child reaches the agreed target (for example, ten stars or tokens), he receives a reward that has been previously agreed upon. The specific application of rewards to exposure assignments is discussed in chapter 8.

Most parents think of rewards as involving candy, presents, or money. These reinforcers do work well and can be an instant prize for young children who need immediate recognition. However, parents and children should be encouraged to consider that material reinforcers are not the *only* effective way of increasing positive and appropriate behavior. Social reinforcers such as verbal praise, hugs and cuddles, and time spent together playing games or sports are excellent ways of reinforcing desired behavior and helping children feel good about themselves. In fact, in our program we try to encourage parents to use these social reinforcers far more than material ones. One reason for this is that social reinforcers provide the extra benefit of increased quality time for the family. Anxiety-related behaviors become the focus of a considerable amount of parental attention, often outweighing that given to any coping behaviors the child may have. Parents often report sheer frustration with the demands made by the child, and guilt at their lack of tolerance. In fact, when some families first appear for treatment, the atmosphere can be very strained. Therefore, any time spent doing pleasant activities as a family will not only provide a reward for the child but also helps the family as a whole. It must be noted, however, that time spent with parents should be age appropriate. Older adolescents, for example, will not usually be interested in quality family time (though they may still be interested in spending time with one or other parent).

Of course, rewards need to be appropriate in size to the difficulty of the task. Surprisingly, we find a small but consistent number of parents who reward inappropriately. First, a very small number of parents will tend to give rewards that are simply too large for the task the child is engaging in. This is often likely to be caused by the parents' feelings of anxiety, unassertiveness, or guilt. Such parents need to be reminded that, hopefully, the child will be earning many rewards in the future and providing excessive rewards too soon will result in difficulty in encouraging the child to continue.

Another problem with rewarding children excessively or inappropriately is that doing so subtly confirms the child's anxieties about the feared situation—it conveys a message to the child that his achievement is extraordinary. These parents may need help in dealing with their own anxieties about what the child is attempting or about what is developmentally and culturally appropriate to expect children to be able to do.

A second, slightly larger proportion of parents simply does not reward enough. They may believe that giving rewards is a form of bribery. In response to this concern, point out the differences between a bribe and a reward: a bribe is when you coerce a child to do something that is beneficial only to yourself and not to the child. A reward is given to the child when he has done something positive for himself.

Some parents protest about giving rewards (or even praise) to their child because they believe their child should know how to behave and should not be rewarded for simply doing as their parents tell them or for doing something that other children can do without difficulty. Discussion of the importance of motivation might help here, as might discussion of the different strengths and weaknesses that various individuals may have. Sometimes, identifying a source of extreme anxiety for the parent (such as standing on stage naked) may help in developing a sense of empathy for the difficulty their child is going through. Remind the parent of the development of anxiety as discussed in chapter 2—anxiety is not simply a voluntary or "naughty" behavior; it is a source of great distress. A focus on verbal and social rewards may help limit any resentment of "unfair advantages" that the child may be receiving.

Finally, some parents do not feel the need to reward their child for completing a task or reaching a goal because they believe the completion of the goal should be reward enough. You could respond by agreeing that reaching a goal is intrinsically rewarding, but younger people need additional incentives to get them started. The child is going to be asked to face situations over the following weeks that cause him extreme distress, so additional reinforcements will be necessary. Young children find it very difficult to be motivated by merely the thought of how good it will feel when it's finished. Again, helping the parent develop some empathy for their child might be valuable.

You may come across some parents who hold on to their beliefs about not rewarding and continue to disagree with the effectiveness of the proposed methods. The child in such a family takes much longer to improve or may resist improvement entirely. To avoid this possibility, perhaps you can arrive at a compromise with the parents. You might encourage them to test out the effectiveness of these methods (including giving rewards) for just a short time and then make a judgment about whether they will continue.

Finally, parents may be concerned about difficulties with siblings who may resent the extra attention and rewards given to the anxious child. Parents can overcome this by instituting a reward program that involves the whole family, such as going on an outing to the beach. In this way, siblings can become involved in encouraging (but not nagging or disparaging) the anxious child.

Ignoring

With this strategy, parents remove their attention from the child's naughty behavior and pay attention again when the child behaves appropriately. This is to be immediately followed by specific praise when the more appropriate behavior is performed. Ignoring is particularly effective for younger children with attention-seeking or naughty behaviors. This strategy is also useful for managing the anxious child's reassurance-seeking behavior. However, it is essential for the parent to clearly explain to the child the nature and the purpose of the ignoring, because otherwise he may feel neglected. The technique of ignoring is not an invitation for parents to be nasty to their child. Ignoring should occur in relation to a specific behavior and in the context of parental warmth and support.

For example, Sally has asked her father if she can watch a television program that she is not allowed to watch as it is not suitable for children her age. Her father responds by saying, "Sally, Mommy and I don't think that is a good program for you to watch. It is a show that is better for older children." Sally asks her father two more times. Her voice becomes louder and whinier. Her father states one more time, in a quiet and soft tone, what he has already said. But Sally persists. "Sally, I have already given you my answer. If you continue to ask me about the TV show I am not going to answer you. I will be happy to talk to you again about what other shows you could watch." Sally starts crying and continues to request that she be allowed to watch the television show. Her father ignores her behavior. Her behavior intensifies, but when she realizes Dad is not going to budge, she begins to calm down. When she is more settled, her father says, "I am happy to talk to you now that you have calmed down. Thanks for calming down. Do you want to talk about another TV show you could watch?"

Reassurance-Seeking Children

Sometimes children are accidentally rewarded for behaving anxiously. This is particularly likely in the context of reassurance-seeking children. Anxious children will often check for reassurance from their parents in every new situation. They may ask their parents about the coming situation over and over again, sometimes for several hours. Signs of distress may in turn elicit the parents' increased physical affection and attempts to provide distraction, both of which are highly rewarding. As a result, children will fail to learn that they can cope with situations themselves and continue to build dependence on their parents, which undermines their self-confidence. Parents need to be made aware of these rewards and need to plan methods of reducing them.

To deal with reassurance-seeking children, parents should be encouraged to set limits on the amount and nature of the questions they are willing to answer in these situations. At all times, the child should be fully informed and included in these decisions. In general, when a child begins to seek reassurance, the parents should explain the situation to the child once, and should then develop a stock phrase ("you know what is going to happen") for any future questions about that situation. The child should be encouraged to try not to ask more than once and should be praised and rewarded for successful restraint. Parents might also try reminding and encouraging their child to use his detective thinking. Again, if this is done, it needs to be done only once, after which parents need to use a stock phrase to encourage the child to go back to his detective-thinking worksheet himself. As the child becomes better at cognitive restructuring, parents may simply point him to the desired way of thinking by asking, for example, "What could you say to yourself that could help you feel less anxious?" or "What would so and so (the young child's detective figure) do?"

For example, Jessica has been very concerned before school every morning that she is going to be late, although she has always arrived at school on time. In the car, Jessica constantly checks with her mother, "What's the time, Mom? Are we going to be late? What if I get into trouble?" So, one day before school, Jessica and her mom make a plan. They fill out a Realistic Thinking worksheet (chapter 5) to help her think about all the other times she has not been late to school. They also think about what happens to other children when they are late. Jessica recalls that other kids only occasionally get into trouble for being late. Jessica and her mother try to think about the worst thing that could happen. Her mother then says to her, "Jessica, this morning if you ask whether we are going to be late or whether you are going to get into trouble I am going to ask you to have a look at your Realistic Thinking sheet. I will not tell you that everything will be okay, like I usually do, because I know that you will be able to answer your own questions. If you ask me more than once I will not listen to your questions until you can tell me what you have written on your sheet."

On the way to school Jessica asks her mother a series of questions about being late. Jessica's mother responds with, "Jessica, have a look at what you wrote down this morning. Remember that if you ask me about being late or getting into trouble again I am not going to listen to you until you can tell me what's written there." Her mom makes no further attempts to tell her that she is not going to be late or that everything will be okay. When Jessica again asks her mother for reassurance, her mother does not respond to her. Jessica asks again, this time sounding more distressed. Her mother finds it really hard not to tell her everything will be okay and that she won't get into trouble. But she continues to wait for Jessica to read from her sheet. Finally, after a few minutes, Jessica gets it out and reads over what she had written earlier in the morning: "I know I am not going to be late because I am hardly ever late to school. Even if I am late nothing really happens anyway. Most kids when they are late don't even get noticed." Jessica's mother responds with, "Jessica, well done! You have managed to answer your own questions. I knew you would be able to do it on your own. I am very proud of you." Note that even now, her mother does not agree with Jessica's fears or provide any other form of reassurance.

Independence

A major focus of child management for anxious children involves teaching parents to encourage their child to be more independent. We use the term "protection trap" to refer to the cycle in which an anxious child elicits increased protection from a caring parent and, in turn, becomes more anxious. Parents need to be informed about the protection trap in a way that does not place blame on them but allows them to discover ways they may be currently maintaining their child's anxiety. To be set free from this cycle, parents need to allow their children to fight their own battles and make their own mistakes without always coming to the rescue. One of the main purposes of your discussion with parents is to give them permission to be tough. They should be encouraged to direct their child toward facing the situation rather than continually allowing her to back out of it. In allowing the child to face anxiety-provoking situations, parents give her the opportunity to learn that the situation was not as scary or as catastrophic as she had originally believed. This technique also gives her the message that she can cope. Many parents will be quite grateful for this advice, because we often hear them say that they know they are too protective but are scared they may hurt their child by pushing too hard. Discussing with the parent appropriate levels and methods of encouragement can be very valuable. In addition, discussing the difference between being supportive versus overprotective can be helpful.

The following steps can be given to parents as a strategy to use in situations where they might experience difficulty not "rescuing" the child.

Step 1: Summarize what the child has said. Check the accuracy of your understanding of the problem—that is, make sure you know what the child actually means. Communicate your empathy with the child in a sympathetic but matter-of-fact way.

Step 2: Summarize the choices open to the child at this point. On the one hand, the child can continue to feel anxious and upset and behave in an anxious manner. On the other hand, she can choose to do something to reduce her anxiety.

Step 3: Prompt the child to generate as many different ideas as possible about what she might do to reduce the anxiety and feel better. Remember, try not to tell your child exactly what to do, but rather help her figure it out for herself. Encourage the child to generate solutions that she can carry out.

Step 4: Praise the child for the ideas that she has generated. Even if the ideas are not actually very useful, praise her for effort. The fact that she is engaging with you in the process of trying to constructively reduce her anxiety is a very positive and important step.

Step 5: Go through each idea or strategy that the child has generated, one by one. For each idea, ask, "What would happen if you did this?" If the child does not identify obvious consequences to a strategy, gently point them out. For instance, you might say, "I wonder if [name a consequence] would happen if you did [name a strategy] to make yourself feel better. What do you think?" Praise the child for trying to generate likely outcomes for each strategy.

Step 6: For each strategy and resulting outcome that has been suggested, ask the child, "How good would this outcome be for you?" Have the child rate each outcome from zero to ten on a scale in which zero represents the most negative outcome and ten represents the most positive.

Step 7: Prompt the child to select the strategy that is most likely to result in a positive outcome and least likely to result in a negative one.

Let parents know that these steps should only be used as a first stage. As the child becomes better at generating his own solutions to problems, his parents should begin to reduce their involvement even more. Eventually, the goal is for children to solve (age-appropriate) problems on their own without any prompts. If parents do not reduce their involvement, the above steps may eventually become a form of reassurance for the child.

For example, Jessica and her mother have been invited to her cousin's fourteenth birthday party. Jessica's mother feels it is very important for her to go to the party, because Jessica is very close to her cousin, Maria, and Maria was really counting on her to be there. However, when they arrive at the party, Jessica refuses to get out of the car and go to the party. Her mother's usual response would be to go in and make an excuse for Jessica and then drive her home. Instead, she sits down next to Jessica in the car and tries to help her work out what to do.

Mother: Jessica, you obviously don't want to go to the party. Can you tell me what is worrying you?

Jessica: No, I just don't want to go.

Mother: Okay, I know that you don't want to go to the party. I would really like you to go and I know Maria would really like you to be there. What is it that you are worried might happen at the party?

Jessica: I don't know ... [a long pause]. Well, I might be kind of worried that I will have to talk to some of Maria's friends. I don't really know them.

Mother: What do you think might happen if you have to talk to her friends?

Jessica: I don't know, maybe that I won't know what to say and I'll look really stupid.

Mother: Okay, now that I know what you are worrying about I can help you work out what to do. I would really like you to go to the party. You could either sit in the car all afternoon and be miserable because I am not driving you all the way back home, *or* you can try and do something to cope with how you are feeling and go to the party.

Jessica: Can't you just drive me back home? I don't want to sit in the car all day.

Mother: No, I am going to the party now. The decision you have to make is what you are going to do. Do you want to give it a go or not?

Jessica: Oh, all right. [Jessica sighs grudgingly.]

Mother:	Okay. Jessica, let's try and think of as many things as we can that could make you feel less worried when you go to the party. What do you think you could do?
Jessica:	Well, I could go and sit by myself in the corner, where no one can see me all afternoon.
Mother:	Well, that's one idea. Let's try and think of as many as we can to start with. What else could you do?
Jessica:	I don't know. Nothing. [Silence.] I guess I could think about the movie that we are going to see tomorrow.
Mother:	Yes, that's an idea. Thinking about the movie would help you take your mind off your worries. You said you were worried about not having anything to talk about with Maria's friends and looking stupid. How might you challenge those thoughts?
Jessica:	Well, I know Maria likes me.
Mother:	Good, Jessica. Do you usually find things to talk about with people?
Jessica:	I suppose I do. I suppose I could talk about the music, 'cause I know Maria likes the same music I do. But, it's just that sometimes there is a big space in the conversation.
Mother:	Okay, let's say there is a break in the conversation. What is the worst thing that could happen?
Jessica:	They could think I'm a real dork.
Mother:	They could, but what would you think of the other kids? Would you think they were stupid if they couldn't think of anything to talk about either?
Jessica:	Well, I guess I wouldn't think anything of them.
Mother:	If you wouldn't think anything of them, why do you think they would think you were stupid?
Jessica:	I guess they wouldn't.
Mother:	Is there anything else you could do or think about?
Jessica:	Well, it's not like I've got to talk to them all the time. I'm sure we will be doing stuff like playing games and things.
Mother:	Okay. We've come up with a few suggestions. Let's see what would probably happen if we tried these things. Your first suggestion was to stay in the car all afternoon. What do you think would happen if you did that?
Jessica:	Maria would be disappointed if I didn't turn up and I'd be bored out of my brain staying in the car.

Mother:	Okay, so what do you think would happen if you tried the second option, hiding in the corner all afternoon?
Jessica:	Boring! But I wouldn't be worried.
Mother:	Okay. What about thinking about the movie tomorrow to take your mind off things?
Jessica:	I guess that would help.
Mother:	Okay, what about thinking that you usually have things to talk about with people and it's unlikely Maria's friends will think you are a dork? If there is a gap in the conversation you wouldn't think badly of the other people, so it's unlikely they'd think badly of you. What would happen if you thought those things?
Jessica:	I guess I'd be less worried.
Mother:	What about reminding yourself that you won't have to be thinking of things to talk about the whole time, because you will be probably playing games?
Jessica:	Yeah, that would make me less worried too. It really isn't as bad as what I had thought.
Mother:	Okay. Out of all the options that we talked about, which ones do you think would have the best outcome for you? Let's rate each of them out of ten, where zero would be really bad and ten would be the best. Okay, staying in the car?
Jessica:	That is not going to help at all and would be really boring. I'll give it a one.
Mother:	What about going into the party but sitting by yourself?
Jessica:	Three. That's a bit better than staying in the car.
Mother:	Yes, it is a bit better, but doesn't help you face your fears. What about using your detective thinking and actually participating in the party and talking to Maria's friends?
Jessica:	That's the harder option. But it's a better one. An eight.
Mother:	That's very good thinking, Jessica. You have been able to come up with a lot of really good options. I know this is really difficult for you. Now let's decide which one of these options you should do right now.
Jessica:	Well, I think the last one we talked about. Just giving it a go. I will try and talk to Maria's friends and remind myself that I usually do okay talking to people and remind myself that Maria likes me. I can also remember that I won't have to talk to them all night because we will be doing things and playing games where I won't have to think of things to talk about.

Mother: Excellent job, Jessica. You have handled this difficult situation really well. Let's go.

Notice that the bottom line here is that Jessica's mother has refused to drive Jessica home and make excuses for her. The help with cognitive restructuring and problem solving should help model for Jessica appropriate ways of thinking. But the key element is that Jessica's mother allows her to face the consequences of her avoidant behavior by allowing her to sit in the car all afternoon and by letting people think poorly of her by not making excuses for her.

Encouraging children's independence is even more important as they enter adolescence, because at this time parents' protection may become more obvious and perhaps more debilitating for many adolescents. In addition to the strategies mentioned above, parents can develop children's independence by spending more quality time with them. Parents may spend a lot of time making demands or requests of their child and no time really talking with them. This can be so easy to overlook in a busy household, especially in a stressed household. Parents should be encouraged to allocate a small portion of their day as "special time" for talking with their child. The time can be spent discussing recent events in which the adolescent behaved courageously in situations they handled that were difficult or that caused them anxiety. The time can also be spent simply discussing the week's events. During this time, parents should focus on giving the child encouragement about their successes and should be genuinely interested and curious about their week. Parents should refrain from giving advice or making requests or demands; they should just listen to their child. Allocating this time on a regular basis will go a long way in strengthening the parent-child relationship and will also encourage the adolescent's independence. Remember, when negotiating this in therapy, the child's input needs to be considered. The child must be part of the decisions regarding whether, when, and how long the special time will be. The decision should not simply be decided for him or it becomes another example of overcontrol.

Modeling

As discussed in chapter 2, a child can learn anxious behaviors by observing others. It is very normal for children to imitate their parent's behavior. However, children pick up both helpful and unhelpful methods of coping, and parents may not be aware of how they may be subtly influencing their child. You may want to encourage parents to think about situations in which they may be modeling anxious and avoidant behavior to their child. Once this concept is introduced, many parents will begin to discuss situations in which they are anxious. If not, the use of words such as "stressed" or "tense" can reduce defensiveness. Also, encourage parents to think of times when they positively influence their child and model coping or courageous behavior. The principles of cognitive restructuring have already been addressed by this point of treatment, so this may be a good time to motivate parents to make use of their restructuring skills in their own anxiety-provoking situations. Parents will be quick to notice that when they start to be less stressed, their child will also imitate less anxious behavior.

If the parent's anxiety is severe and unmanageable, individual treatment may be necessary. Treatment-outcome research has shown that anxious children with anxious parents show greater improvements when the parent also receives treatment for anxiety (Cobham, Dadds, and Spence 1998).

Nonphysical Punishment

Punishment of oppositional or unwanted behaviors is generally not an important strategy in the treatment of anxious children. These children will commonly be excessively eager to please and are often very sensitive to any form of punishment. Nevertheless, all children can be difficult at times and parents may benefit from a brief coverage of strategies for punishment. Given that the punishment procedures mentioned here are of more value for children with oppositional problems, we will discuss them only briefly—the interested reader is referred to Sanders and Dadds (1993) for more information.

Time-out is one effective form of punishment for children up to around nine years of age that does not involve any physical aggression. When a child misbehaves, he is removed from the presumably rewarding or pleasant situation he is in and placed in a safe but uninteresting environment for a set period of time. It is essential that the terms of time-out be carefully explained to the child. He should know in advance that misbehaving will result in being sent to time-out for a set period (for example, five minutes) and that when the time is up he will be given another opportunity to behave appropriately. The requirements for ending the time-out must also be fully explained. Contingencies for further misbehavior must also be carefully explained to the child, such as a further period in time-out or removal of a privilege.

Removing privileges is another effective punishment, particularly for older children and adolescents. Again, the child needs to be aware of the terms of this arrangement in advance (or at least during the time she is misbehaving). The parent informs the child that if she continues to misbehave, one of her privileges will be removed. For example, she may not be allowed to watch television for a set time or to attend a social outing. If the child continues to misbehave, the parents needs to follow through with their intentions and not use this method merely as a threat (more on this below, under Consistency).

In a small proportion of families there may actually be very few positives in the child's life at all; finding privileges to remove may be quite difficult. Clearly, for these families, implementing punishment in the form of removal of privileges is not the most appropriate strategy. The first step would be to instigate some noncontingent positives in the child's life. For example, the parent and child could set aside time to go for a walk together or do an activity the child enjoys. The focus in child management in these cases should be on the use of rewards to increase the child's desired behaviors rather than punishment.

You'll want to point out to parents that punishing negative behavior is aimed at decreasing the likelihood of that behavior recurring, whereas giving rewards to positive behaviors is aimed at increasing the positive behavior.

Rewarding positive behaviors is generally more useful for children with anxiety, as the anxious child is less likely to have severe behavioral problems and less likely to be in need of punishment.

For example, Sally has been watching television for the past half hour. It is now dinnertime and her mother asks her to come to the dinner table. Sally ignores her mother and continues to watch the television. Her mother repeats her request in the same tone as before. She also states that if Sally does not come to the table she will have to go to the time-out room for five minutes. She continues to watch TV. "Sally, you are going to time-out now for five minutes because you did not come to the table when I asked." Her mother takes her to the time-out room for five minutes. Once the five minutes has ended, Sally's mother returns and asks her if she would like to come to the dinner table. She still refuses to come to the table. "I am going to ask you again. If you do not do what I ask then there will be no television tomorrow afternoon. Sally, would you please come and sit at the table for dinner?" Sally gets up from the chair and walks to the table. Her mom responds, "Thank you for doing as I asked."

It is most effective if this interchange comes in the context of a generally positive relationship. At the first opportunity, her mom should praise Sally for any positive behavior that she notices. In addition, when Sally next comes to the table when asked, her mom should praise the behavior and reward it.

Here's another example. Simon has been more irritable and resistant in recent weeks. He has been getting into a lot of arguments with his younger brother Andre, usually because Simon teases him. His mother has sat him down and talked to him about this and asked him to stop teasing Andre. On this occasion, his mother is outside and hears Simon inside the house teasing his younger brother. She calls to him from outside.

Mother: Simon, give it a break. Please stop hassling your brother.

(Simon ignores his mother. So she walks inside to find him still teasing Andre.)

Mother: Simon, I asked you to stop teasing. If this behavior continues you will not be allowed to go over to John's place tomorrow as you had planned.

Simon: Oh … come on mom, don't be so mean. We're just playing.

(His mother leaves the room only to find that when she walks back outside, Simon starts up the teasing again. She walks back inside.)

Mother: Simon, you did not do as I asked. You continued teasing Andre. You will not be going to John's house tomorrow.

Simon: Oh Mom, come on. Don't be unfair. Please? I won't do it again. I've stopped now.

Mother: No, Simon.

(The next day, Simon asks his mother to drive him to John's place.)

Mother:	Simon, if you had stopped teasing Andre yesterday when I asked, I would be happy to take you to John's, but because you didn't listen to me you are not allowed to go over there.
Simon:	I promised that I wouldn't do it again and I haven't hassled him since then. Please, Mom.
Mother:	No.

Simon complains. But his mother does not respond. He storms off to his bedroom. Again, finding a positive to reward at a near point in the future is important in this situation so that Simon learns that not only are negative behaviors punished, but positives are rewarded. Note that the least effective way to deliver instructions is to call them out, as Simon's mother did at the beginning of this example. A more effective way is to speak directly to the child face-to-face.

Consistency

Consistency is another essential component to behavior management and possibly the most difficult for parents to execute. Parents are likely to be familiar with the principles of child management but argue that the principles are not effective with *their* child. The most common reason for the failure of these strategies is lack of consistency. The child *must* be rewarded and punished consistently. The child should understand that certain behaviors lead to desirable consequences and others lead to undesirable consequences. That said, being consistent 100 percent of the time is very hard work and near impossible. However, if parents work toward improving their consistency in the application of the above strategies, they can help their child behave less anxiously. Encourage parents to identify particular situations in which they may be inconsistent and discuss strategies that would assist them in improving their consistency. The most common ways parents are inconsistent with their application of discipline are through empty threats, accidental rewards, vague instructions, and inconsistency between parents.

Empty Threats

When a child is misbehaving, parents frequently threaten their child with punishments that are not likely to be carried out. This is a very common mistake that almost all parents are guilty of. Giving empty threats reduces the potency of future parental requests. This can be a problem in terms of rewards as well. Parents may plead with a child to complete a particular task and offer a reward that they later forget or are unable to carry out, which, again, reduces the potency of future requests. For greater effectiveness, parents need to follow through with the reinforcements and punishments they threaten.

Accidental Rewards

Accidental rewards are given when parents give in to a screaming or whining child. The child learns that screaming or whining will eventually lead to obtaining what he desires. Thus, the next time a child is denied a request, he will persist by screaming and whining until the parent loses patience and he obtains his request. This is also true for giving reassurance to a child who is constantly seeking it. As discussed earlier, limits must be set on reassurance-seeking behavior so as not to create a false sense of security for the child. When a parent gives in to a child who is constantly seeking reassurance despite the limits that have been set, he learns to continue questioning to receive the reassurance.

Vague Instructions

When parents are not specific in the instructions they give their child, those instructions are far less likely to be carried out properly. For example, asking the child to "relax" or "calm down" is not as specific as, "Try to think of all the times you have gone to sleep and nothing bad has happened," or "Try thirty seconds of your relaxation." Similarly, after a parent says, "I want you to go to school today," the child may go to school but only stay for an hour. In a strict sense the child has obeyed her parent's request.

Inconsistency between Parents

Parents should discuss and agree on the behaviors they believe to be appropriate for their child, because inconsistencies between parents complicate the child's treatment. For example, Sally is afraid of catching the bus to school. If one parent has been encouraging her to take the bus but the other gives in and drives her to school, a far greater time will be required for her fear to be reduced. Again, this is one reason why both parents should attend treatment, if possible. If this is not possible, the parent attending must communicate in detail the strategies discussed in the session.

Inconsistency between parents is quite common. A valuable exercise for parents is to identify those situations in which they find it more difficult to be consistent and work together to determine the situation they are each more able to handle. Most often, parents find that the times they are least consistent are the times when they feel most stressed. When parents are tired, angry, or anxious, they are likely to be far less patient with their child. Ideally, when parents recognize that they might be feeling stressed, they should withdraw from the situation and return when they are more able to be consistent and calm. Again, they should inform the child of what they are doing and why. For example, "Simon, I am feeling pretty stressed right now. It is important to me that we finish this exercise together. But I think I need to have a break for a little while so that I can settle down and give you my full attention another time." This way, the parent minimizes the possibility of the child feeling rejected or unwanted. This behavior also models a useful coping strategy.

This point also raises the issue of the relationship between the parents. We have had great success in treating anxious children even in cases of marital distress, but the key issue is consistency. To some extent, the parents' relationship is not of great importance in terms of dealing with their child's anxiety as long as they can put aside their differences sufficiently to agree on how they will handle their child. Where relationship difficulties interfere with this consistency, the child is likely to experience problems and the parental relationship may need to be made the focus of therapy.

Practice

Parents should be encouraged to start putting into practice the strategies that have been discussed in this chapter. Make it clear to parents that you will be monitoring the progress of their skills, and inform them that these strategies become even more important in the following weeks when their child begins to face feared situations. If parents are struggling with particular aspects of child management, the effectiveness of the exposure tasks may be reduced.

Encourage parents to complete sample exercises 7 and 8. Parents are expected to recall an occasion when their child successfully completed a task or did something that the parents were pleased with, and then write down the praise and the reward they gave their child. Recommend that parents make at least one entry on the form per day. In the next session, carefully go through the entries with the parents and encourage their efforts as well as point out areas that need improving. In addition, ask the parents to recall a situation during the week when their child was *not* rewarded or praised for doing something positive. Parents can then brainstorm ways they could have praised and rewarded their child. Group programs provide an excellent opportunity for feedback and brainstorming.

On sample exercise 8, parents are to make note of occasions when their child was naughty and, as honestly as possible, write down how they dealt with the situation and what happened as a result of their action. When you go through the exercise with the parents in the following session, encourage them to look for any relationships between their responses and the child's subsequent behavior. You may point out instances when they have used the strategies effectively and occasions when they have been less successful. You may wish to reenact the event with the parents and provide feedback and further suggestions.

Dealing with Difficulties

Independence

Some parents will experience difficulty allowing their child to become more independent, sometimes because of extreme overinvolvement in one or both parents. During therapy sessions, you may notice that a parent will often

Sample Exercise 7:
Praising and Rewarding My Child

Date	What is it that my child did? (Behavior)	What praise did I give my child? (Praise)	What reward did I give my child? (Reward)

Sample Exercise 8:
Dealing with My Child's Negative Behaviors

Date	What is it that my child did? (Behavior)	What action did I take?	What happened when I did this?

answer questions for their child, talk over him, or jump in to fix the situation if he is having trouble. If you notice that a parent has trouble releasing some control, it may be necessary to continually remind the parent of the importance of their child's independence: "It would really be great to hear Jason answer this question himself since it is important that we start to encourage him to have confidence in his own ideas." This initially gentle confrontation may gradually become more overt and directed over time if the parents seem unable to gain insight or are unwilling to let go. With more direct confrontation, you'll need to outline, in detail, specific examples from within sessions (that you have observed) as well as from their daily life (that the family has described to you). Ultimately, if change does not seem to come, you may need to directly point out the harmful effect that the parents' behavior is having on the child and inform them that the child will not improve as long as they continue to control him.

For some families, assisting the parents in encouraging independence in their child will become a major focus of treatment. First, identify the reasons the parents are experiencing difficulties releasing some control over the child. Perhaps they are trying to avoid the increased anxiety they experience when they do allow their child to be more independent. If this is the case, the cognitive behavioral strategies that have been applied to the child can also be applied to the parents. They'll need to begin by identifying what it is they are worried about happening if the child is given more independence, and then gather evidence for how likely it is that their fears will come true. Use the cognitive restructuring sheets in chapter 5 to guide the process. In addition to the restructuring, parents may be encouraged to develop an exposure hierarchy to enable them to allow their child greater independence. Begin by encouraging the parent to identify areas where they think they need to develop their child's independence, and then ask them to rate each of these areas in order of difficulty. For example, allowing the child to hand in her school homework without checking it first might cause them the least anxiety, and allowing the child to stay overnight at a friend's house might be the most difficult. The parents should begin with the easiest option—carrying it out will be their homework for that week. Once they feel they have been able to carry out the task with reduced anxiety, move on to the next challenge. In the following chapter there will be more information on developing hierarchies for situations that cause the child anxiety. The same principles apply to developing exposure hierarchies for parents.

In some cases, a parent may also unintentionally or even intentionally undermine the child's attempts at independence. Perhaps the child's dependence satisfies a need in the parent such as company, increased affection, or empathy. In this case, once the motivating factor is identified you may need to gently confront the parent with your hypothesis and suggest that this may be hindering the child's progress. If gentle confrontation and insight do not work, confrontation may need to gradually be increased. You may need to allocate additional session time or perhaps refer the parent to a therapist to discuss these needs and how they could be met differently. The parents may also have irrational beliefs about what will happen to them if their child becomes more independent. Again, cognitive restructuring techniques may be beneficial to challenge these beliefs.

Consistency

Being consistent is one of the most difficult aspects of parenting. Once parents have tried some of the methods discussed in this chapter, they will often report that it "just didn't work." You will need to examine in a step-by-step fashion what happened when they used the strategy, and try to identify any points where they could have improved their effectiveness. For example, the parents may have told their daughter that if she sleeps in her own room for the whole night, she will be rewarded with a special treat after dinner the next night. The parents report that their daughter slept in her own room the first night but then wanted to sleep in their bed the following night. When you query the parents about the reward, you may find out that it was not given to the child the next night but promised for another evening instead. Such problems are especially pronounced in families that lead very chaotic lives. In families where both parents are overcommitted and there are several children, it may be difficult for the parents to deliver rewards (especially those that involve time) as promised. Strongly emphasize the importance of consistency to the parents. Let them know that there is little point in continuing with the program unless they are willing to make a serious commitment. They may also need your help in selecting rewards that they have the ability to deliver.

The Child's Behavior Is Worse

Parents may report that although they applied your strategies correctly and consistently, their child's behavior worsened. Letting parents know that this is a common feature of a successful program can help relieve any concerns. When the rules in a family change, children will test out the new limits and may push their parents a little further in an attempt to see how serious the parents are about the changes. Parents need to be urged to persist until the child realizes that Mom and Dad are serious about these new rules.

Warn parents of this possibility ahead of time. Praise them for applying the strategies consistently and correctly, and tell them that if they stick with the program improvements will be observed in the near future.

Parent Relationship Difficulties

Your initial interview should have covered the topic of the parents' relationship. If you observe increased tension or arguing between the parents, you may need to make a decision about what you believe to be the treatment priority—either the child's anxiety or the parents' relationship issues. If you think the parents' relationship is the primary concern, you should consider shifting the focus of therapy to deal with their relationship for a period or referring them to a couple therapist. At this point, you should discuss your decision with the family and air your concerns about their treatment progress. Inform them that you believe their child's treatment is being hindered by the difficulties they are experiencing in their relationship. Parents may choose to spend time working on their relationship before returning to your program with their child.

If you think the child's anxiety is more of a treatment priority, then of course the decision should be made to continue therapy. However, before treatment continues, some guidelines should be put in place for the remaining therapy sessions. For example, the parents may be asked to use the therapy sessions to focus on devising strategies to decrease the child's anxiety rather than spending the time arguing with each other. You may want to suggest that whenever they begin arguing about something you view as irrelevant to the agreed treatment goal of reducing the child's anxiety, you will interrupt and bring them back to the task at hand.

The content of the arguments that parents bring to the sessions may at times be relevant to the child's treatment. In this case, the issues need to be discussed and dealt with. For example, the family may argue during the session about how the child's anxiety is managed. This is the case for Jason's parents. They have differing views on which strategies they should utilize to manage Jason's rituals. Jason's father thinks he should just forget about the problem and it will go away with time. His mother, on the other hand, is unhappy with the support she is getting from her husband and wishes he would help her more with managing Jason's rituals. In this scenario, you would explain to Jason's father that ignoring his rituals completely is very unlikely to help. You can also explain to Jason's mother the long-term effects of being too involved with his rituals. When parents express reluctance to change, point out to them that the strategies they have been using up until now have not been successful in reducing the child's anxiety and trying something different might be worthwhile as an experiment. The parents can be given the option of trying out the strategies that you know are effective in reducing anxiety both in the short term and in the long term. You can negotiate a deal with the parents: if the strategies you suggest are not successful, the situation can be reevaluated in several weeks.

If the parents decide that they want to continue treating their child's anxiety and they are still having difficulties controlling their arguments during the session, you may want to propose that only one parent attend the treatment sessions at a time, alternating every week. This is really a last resort; it should only be used if all other efforts to reduce the parents' arguing during the session has failed. If this option is taken, there needs to be a serious attempt to ensure that the absent parent is briefed on the main issues covered that session. You might want to tape the sessions so that the absent parent can listen to them, or you might want to provide detailed notes.

Parent-Child Relationship Difficulties

In families where there is a lot of conflict between parent and child, you may find that treatment progress is not as smooth as planned. This is uncommon among anxious families, but does occur in cases of comorbid externalizing problems. In many cases, there may be some secondary anger and resentment as a result of the interference caused by the anxiety. Trying to get the family to simply set aside their differences is the best method, because the anger will usually lift once gains become apparent.

As in the case of parental conflict, if the conflict between parent and child seems to be interfering with therapeutic progress, you may need to reconsider whether anxiety management is the most appropriate goal at this point or whether the parent-child conflict is more pressing. You may need to allocate some time to resolve the conflicts within the family and equip the family with problem-solving strategies to deal with future conflicts that arise. The first step toward resolution is identifying the area of conflict and making sure all members involved are given an uninterrupted opportunity to tell their side of the story. Make sure that each person involved in the conflict has been heard and that you have accurately understood what has been said. Clarify for the family that they have the option of continuing to argue and fight with each other over this issue, *or*, together, they can decide to work out a better solution to the problem. The next step is to encourage each family member to generate as many solutions to the problem as they can. Tell them you need to hear everyone's solutions regardless of how unhelpful they may seem. Write down each of the possible solutions. Once the family has exhausted every possibility, go through each of the solutions generated one by one. Ask all the family members what they think would happen if each option was chosen. You may need to assist the family in thinking of all of the possible consequences for each option. Once the options have been covered, have each family member rate from zero to ten all of the options, and ask the family to choose the option (or combination of options) that would be most likely to result in a positive outcome for everyone. As facilitator of this process, you need to make sure that each family member has the opportunity to have their options heard and discussed. At times you may need to interrupt the parents' discussion and give the child the opportunity to give her opinion.

Although a conflict-ridden family may also be very busy and may have little time to spend with the child, emphasize to the parents the therapeutic benefit of spending time participating in activities of the child's choice. This time should be planned and scheduled into both the parents' and the child's days, and the time should be devoted purely to the child. The child needs to understand that this is her "special time." There may be many excuses from busy parents. If this is the case, sit them down for a discussion of the goals of treatment and life priorities. Explain to the parents that the time does not need to be long—we have seen families in which as few as fifteen minutes per day produced a marked difference in the relationship. For adolescents, this time can be even more spaced—say, a half hour to an hour once per week.

Chapter 8

Exposure

What Is Exposure?

The term "exposure" refers to a variety of specific techniques that all involve bringing the subject into contact with the feared stimulus. Some of the specific terms include "graded exposure," "systematic desensitization," and "flooding." We use the generic term "exposure" to reflect the belief that all of these specific strategies are probably working via a common mechanism. A full discussion of possible mechanisms of exposure is beyond the scope of this book; suffice it to say that exposure allows children to learn that the feared stimuli are in fact not threatening and that they can cope with them (Foa and McNally 1996, 327–341; Williams 1996, 344–368). Arguably, exposure is the single most important treatment strategy for the reduction of anxiety in both adults and children.

The basic principle is to encourage the child to face the situations he fears and avoids—long enough and often enough that he eventually becomes used to them. Exposure to feared situations gives him opportunities to practice different ways of behaving and learn different ways of coping with fear. In order to increase the chance of compliance and improve its acceptability, the exposure is usually graded. This means that less frightening situations are dealt with first; only when these are mastered are more difficult situations attempted. The same principles apply to all types of fears, whether the fears are manifested as separation anxiety, specific phobia, or social phobia.

We conceptualize exposure as an extension of the cognitive restructuring discussed in the previous chapter: learning logically and intellectually that certain events are not really so terrible and that one can cope with them can be reinforced and extended by directly experiencing the event. Obviously, the child will need to gain some degree of competence in cognitive restructuring before beginning exposure. This does not mean that the child needs to be completely competent at realistic thinking—in fact, some children will never master this skill. For many children, exposure strategies will succeed where the more intellectual cognitive restructuring fails. In addition, cognitive restructuring will never provide complete control for anxiety, so all children will need to extend these principles through exposure. However, those children who can master realistic thinking are likely to do even better with exposure. Deciding consciously that a particular situation is not threatening and then directly experiencing that situation is a very powerful way of combating anxiety. Along similar lines, mastery of relaxation principles can provide the child with the skill of managing excessive anxiety in frightening situations, which helps turn the exposure into a positive experience.

The Key Principles of Exposure

Exposure is a commonsense approach that appears logical to children and their parents. Many parents may have tried elements of this process in their endeavors to deal with their child's anxiety in the past. However, lack of knowledge and their own anxieties may have stopped them from applying it consistently or extensively (more on this at the end of the chapter, under Dealing with Difficulties). There are three basic principles.

- Fears are faced gradually, working from slightly difficult to the most difficult. A list, referred to as a hierarchy, is drawn up to cover a range of feared or difficult situations. The child attempts each one in turn beginning with the least difficult, and experiences gradual increases in the level of difficulty and anxiety as she progresses through the list.

- The child must stay in the feared situation long enough to learn that the bad things she fears will not happen. During the exposure program, the child should experience some difficult situations and learn that although she initially felt anxious and uncomfortable, the bad things she feared did not actually happen. Ideally, the child will stay in the situation until she is no longer scared, although such a scenario is not always practical. The child should at least stay long enough to confirm that her negative belief is not true. If the child pulls out of the exercise before her belief is proved false, her anxiety will not reduce and may even be increased.

- Practice and repetition are the keys to success. Engaging a situation without mishap just once can be too easily attributed to luck or some other unpredictable process. The child must repeat the process so many times that she gradually learns the situation itself is not threatening. This may mean many repetitions of similar steps on the hierarchy until she feels a real mastery of the problem. Anxious children may have developed subtle ways of avoiding situations and may report diminished anxiety simply to "look good." You as well as the child's parents need to be aware of this.

Explaining Reality Testing to Parents

Parents need advice and, at times, active coaching to allow their child to try something that may have caused anxiety in the past. If parents are anxious, time should be spent helping them, as well as the child, think realistically about the possible consequences. Parents may have anxieties about their child's capacity to tolerate a particular level of anxiety and discomfort, and/or they may feel that their child is more sensitive than other children. They need encouragement and support in allowing the child to attempt the exposure without stepping in to rescue him. If the parent herself also fears a particular situation, she should be encouraged to also attempt exposure, either with the child or separately, in order to model to the child successful control of fear.

There may be differences between parents regarding what is reasonable and realistic for a child that age to attempt or be responsible for. These differences between parents need acknowledgment and discussion so that the child receives a clear and consistent message from both parents. This is particularly important when one parent is overly protective and involved or when both parents do not live with the child. All of the child-management principles from the previous chapter are relevant here. Further parenting issues are discussed under Dealing with Difficulties.

Remember that what you will be asking your clients to do will be difficult for the parents as well as the child. Anyone who is a parent knows how painful it is to stand by while your child is afraid. The first urge for most parents will be to leap in and help their child get through the situation without distress. Yet this is exactly what you are telling them not to do. This will be tough for all parents—for some, it will be next to impossible. To help the process, talk with the parents in advance about their likely feelings of helplessness and guilt when they urge their child to undertake difficult tasks. Letting them know this is normal and expected will help them deal with these feelings more easily. You might also discuss ways in which they can cope with these feelings if and when they arise. Brainstorm some strategies, such as distraction, realistic thinking, or social support, by which the parent who is involved in the exposure can help reduce her own negative feelings.

Explaining Reality Testing to Children

Children will need careful explanation of the graded exposure process and what they will be expected to do. After all, you are going to be asking them to do some pretty unpleasant things. Currently, when they are feeling anxious, their automatic response is to avoid. You will be asking them to break this comfortable pattern. That said, we're always interested to see how many children understand the logic of exposure and are willing to try it, at least in principle.

Children can be taught the concepts of exposure by using examples of a hypothetical child facing a situation that is both frightening and desirable. Your child's task is to draw up a plan to help the hypothetical child reach the desired goal and overcome his fears by gradually becoming used to the situation. Some examples are provided below. Generally, you'll want to begin by using very concrete examples of simple fears to clearly demonstrate the principle of a step-by-step increase in levels of difficulty.

For Younger Children:

Tony is scared of the water but wants to go swimming with his friends.

Katie hates heights but really wants to go to her best friend's birthday party in a restaurant on top of a very tall building.

Jeff won't play in the park or the garden in case a spider lives there.

The therapist is afraid of heights but needs to climb a very tall ladder to clean leaves off the roof.

For Adolescents:

Sonia has to get up in front of the whole school to make an announcement and is very scared.

Joanna has to attend camp with the school band. She worries about being away from home for so long.

Tony feels embarrassed eating in front of other people in case he spills something. His class is going out to dinner at a restaurant.

Applying the Process of Exposure to a Simple Problem

To explain the ideas involved in exposure to children, first use an example of a less complex problem such as the simple phobias mentioned above to provide a concrete and easily understood overview of how the process will work.

This activity can most effectively be done as a brainstorming exercise on a large sheet of paper. On one side of the paper, draw a figure in the current situation—such as Katie, who wishes to overcome her fear of heights—to outline the problem and on the other side draw the desired goal—the party in the high restaurant.

Engage the child by providing him with a marker to add his ideas of some steps between these points. At this stage, don't worry about the steps being out of order. If necessary, prompt some suggestions, especially at the lower and middle range of difficulty. Once the child has generated as many steps as he can, ask him whether Katie could now perform each of these steps to learn not to be frightened. This discussion raises two important issues. First, are the steps practical? Are they things that Katie could really do, or are they too fanciful (such as going up in a hot air balloon)? Any steps that are impractical should be removed. Next, discuss the size of the steps. If Katie manages a particular step, would that allow her to move to the next step fairly easily, or are some of the steps too far apart? If the child feels that some steps are too far apart, extra steps need to be added between them. The final result becomes the exposure stepladder. At this point, the child might also wish to mention some detective thinking points.

Next, ask the child to predict what the levels of anxiety would be for the person attempting these steps using a worry scale (figure 5, chapter 4)—how would that person feel before trying a step, during the step, and afterward? This discussion can be used to illustrate the principle of reductions in anxiety over time in the situation and the reductions in anxiety for higher steps as lower steps become easier.

To explain this further to adolescents, you may wish to draw up a rough graph to illustrate a reduction of anxiety levels during exposure to the feared situation and, with further trials, a reduction in initial levels of anxiety and a quicker tapering off of anxiety levels. It is important to predict that the reduction in anxiety will not be a smooth process; there may be hiccups or setbacks along the way.

Finally, you will need to emphasize to the child the importance of staying in a situation long enough for fears to reduce. Ask the child what would happen if a step were done very quickly—for example, if Tony, who is afraid of learning to swim, jumped in the pool and got out right away, what would happen to him the next time he tried going in the water? What would he have learned? Use this discussion to emphasize the points of gradual steps in the exposure process and the importance of staying in the situation long enough to feel safe and to know that nothing bad will happen. Point out that anxious children will often avoid a problem by rushing through the situation and so avoid experiencing both the anxiety *and* a reduction of anxiety levels. These children have not effectively tested their fears and so remain sensitized to the situation.

Forming a Fears and Worries List

The next step in the exposure process is to develop a list of specific situations that the child either finds difficult or actually avoids through various well-developed strategies. This list of difficult situations forms the basis for selecting target areas for exposure.

At this stage of the process getting parents involved with younger children is very valuable. The parents and child should work together to brainstorm a range of feared situations. However, you'll need to monitor that the parents are only helping and are not taking over for the child. This is a good opportunity for overinvolved parents to practice helping their child without inhibiting their independence. Adolescents should be encouraged to take responsibility for their own hierarchy. Some children will be unable to nominate or suggest problem areas or may even suddenly claim to have no problems at all. If this occurs, and you believe the child is avoiding her fears, challenge her to do it anyway. After all, if she really doesn't fear the situation, exposure to it should be an easy way to get a reward! If the child does admit to the problems but refuses to tackle them, allow her to work on one area and plan to try the other, more difficult, problems later. If children have early successes in the program to build their confidence, more difficult situations later on will appear more manageable.

Watch to see that the items are realistic. For example, few people can achieve a goal of *never* being anxious in exams or of being the most popular person in school. Help both child and parents set realistic and achievable goals that are consistent with what most children of that age would be able to do.

Once the child has generated a list of feared situations and events, help her write a Fears and Worries List by dividing the situations and events into low, medium, and high worry categories and assigning a value of zero to ten from the worry scale.

Sample Exercise 9:
Fears and Worries List

These things are <u>really</u> hard to do   **Worry Scale**
                                                                  0–10

_____

_____

_____

_____

_____

_____

These things are hard to do

_____

_____

_____

_____

_____

_____

These things make me a little worried

_____

_____

_____

_____

_____

_____

This list will assist you and the child in choosing which situations to select as a focus for the first attempts at exposure. The other situations will be the focus of exposure hierarchies to be worked on later. Here is Jessica's initial list.

Jessica's Fears and Worries List

	Situation	Worry Scale
High	Having an injection	10
	Teacher yelling at me	9
	Making mistakes in tests	8
	Falling over and getting hurt at school	8
	Forgetting my homework	8
	Seeing my blood	9
	Thinking about burglars	8
	Hearing noises outside	9
	Getting bad marks	9
	Going to new places	8
Medium	Being late for school	7
	Forgetting library books	7
	Giving the wrong answer in class	7
	Making mistakes in my homework	7
	Doing messy work at school	8
	Seeing other people's blood	6
	Giving a formal talk at school	5
	Meeting new people	6
Low	Being at the doctor's office for my sister's appointment	4
	Chatting at school	4

Developing an Exposure Stepladder

The next step in the process is to begin to develop one or more specific exposure "stepladders"—hierarchies. First, the child should select one problem area from the Fears and Worries List to focus on. Guide his choice toward a problem in the lower range of difficulty to maximize the probability of success and enhance confidence and hope about the treatment. A separate hierarchy should be created for each broad problem area. What constitutes a "problem area"? There is no single answer to this, and it is not really important anyway. Hierarchies are simply a way of organizing and structuring exposure exercises in a systematic and consistent way. Any situations that logically fit together could be considered an "area." For example, a child may include fear of sleeping at a friend's house and fear of sleeping at a relative's house in the hierarchy for sleeping away from home. Fear of going to school might be more logically placed in a separate hierarchy. A child may have one, two, or several hierarchies going simultaneously.

The hierarchy should cover the whole range of situations relating to the problem selected—from something the child is *almost* able to achieve now to a situation that is well beyond his current capacity. There is no set number of steps to be included between these extremes, but there should be enough to provide plenty of opportunities for practice. A large number of small steps is most effective and helps reinforce the learning. Large steps and big jumps in the level of difficulty between items should be avoided. Each situation chosen should be clearly specified with details of time to be spent, the place, and what is to be achieved. The inclusion of rewards will be discussed later in this chapter, in the section titled Deciding on Rewards.

You may determine that the list includes some more difficult situations that will need to be broken into smaller, less daunting steps. You'll also need to make sure that the steps are practical, realistic, and appropriate. Steps that require lots of resources, time, or effort may be necessary occasionally but should not be included too often. Encourage the use of everyday activities—if the tasks are too elaborate or difficult to organize or demand special efforts from parents, they are less likely to be completed.

With your help (and with the parents' help, in the case of younger children), the child should list the steps in order of difficulty, from step one up to the top, most difficult, step. Including the parents will help ensure that the steps are possible in terms of parental time and resources, and commits the parents to the task. Adolescents will usually be able to devise their own hierarchies with peer or therapist assistance. In a group setting, the other participants may be helpful in brainstorming some possible steps. Before involving the parents directly, talk with the adolesent about what sort of parental help he might need. At the very least, most parents should be aware of what their adolescents are attempting to do so that they can provide encouragement and rewards.

Sally's Exposure Hierarchy (Separation Anxiety Disorder)

Sally's anxiety about staying at a friend's house to play was selected as the target for her first exposure task, because she rated it low to medium on her worry scale. Its relatively low rating meant she was more likely to achieve some success with this problem, which would be highly rewarding and could be extrapolated to her difficulties with other separations.

Sally's goal: To be able to play at a friend's house without worrying about being away from Mom.

Exposure Stepladder:

1. While at her friend's house with Mom, Mom leaves for ten minutes.

2. While at her friend's house with Mom, Mom leaves for thirty minutes.

3. Mom drops her off at her friend's house and Sally plays there alone for one hour.

4. Plays there alone for two hours.

5. Repeat the previous step with a different friend at a different house.

6. Attend Nancy's birthday party.

7. Eat dinner with a friend's family.

Jessica's Exposure Hierarchy (Specific Phobia)

This example highlights the importance of having a good working relationship with other professionals, because Jessica's working with her fear of going to the doctor required the cooperation of the family doctor. The goal of treatment in this case was not to make Jessica feel completely at ease with injections, but to get her to the point where she could tolerate them.

Jessica's goal: To visit the doctor without excessive fear and to tolerate having injections.

Exposure Stepladder:

1. Stand outside the office for five minutes.

2. Walk into the waiting room and sit on a seat.

3. Sit in the waiting room for ten minutes.

4. Talk to the doctor in the waiting room.

5. Sit with Mom in the office while the doctor talks to Mom.

6. Have a physical examination with Mom there.

7. Sit in the office and hold a needle for several minutes.

8. Hold the point of the needle against her skin.

9. Allow the doctor to hold the point of the needle against her skin.

10. Have an injection.

Jessica's Exposure Hierarchy (Generalized Anxiety Disorder)

One of Jessica's main areas of difficulty was her tendency to be a perfectionist. In operational terms, Jessica avoided the possibility of making mistakes. Therefore, an exposure hierarchy was developed with the goal of exposing Jessica to the possibility (and sometimes the actuality) of making mistakes in order to learn that nothing catastrophic would happen.

Jessica's goal: Not to be bothered by making mistakes at school.

Sample Exercise 10:
My Exposure Stepladder

I want to _____

_____

_____

Step 6 _____

_____

My reward _____

Step 5 _____

_____

My reward _____

Step 4 _____

_____

My reward _____

Step 3 _____

_____

My reward _____

Step 2 _____

_____

My reward _____

Step 1 _____

_____

My reward _____

Exposure Stepladder:

1. Listen to music for half an hour before doing homework after school.

2. Cross out a mistake in homework and hand it in without rewriting it.

3. Do not bring a permission note back to school on the first day it is due.

4. Make a deliberate mistake in a math exercise.

5. Draw a doodle in the margin of a page that will be turned in.

6. Hand in an essay with two spelling mistakes.

7. Answer a question in class without being 100 percent sure of the answer.

8. Forget to take library books to school on library day.

9. Deliberately give the wrong answer to a question.

10. Don't have the correct textbook for a lesson.

Children with generalized anxiety disorder have a broad range of fears, and their worries may also appear to change over time as they become focused on other issues. Even though some of the worries can appear vague and broad ranging, there are usually a number of specific concerns that can be a target for effective exposure. Worries about making mistakes, being late, being assertive, and coping with new situations are common concerns for children with GAD. These situations can all be structured into a step-by-step exposure hierarchy as in Jessica's example above.

Children who worry about genuinely catastrophic events such as war or AIDS will still respond well to exposure to the cues that trigger these worries. For example, children who worry about such topics may avoid watching the news or reading about current events. This avoidance behavior can be made the focus of exposure. At the same time, the child and parents should be encouraged to acknowledge that bad things *do* sometimes happen in the world, and to think realistically about the likelihood of these things occurring to them.

Jason's Exposure Hierarchy (Obsessive-Compulsive Disorder) #1

Jason's concerns about cleanliness and germs extended to a number of related areas and required several exposure hierarchies. One of these hierarchies was directed at his fear of eating foods that might possibly contain germs.

Jason's goal: To eat food in different places without worrying.
Exposure Stepladder:

1. Watch his mother make a sandwich and eat it without checking for "off" bits.

2. Eat a sandwich his mother makes without watching her make it.

3. Eat some cake at his grandmother's house.

4. Eat some snack food at his best friend's house.

5. Eat lunch at his best friend's house.

6. Buy lunch from the school cafeteria.

7. Eat a hamburger at a fast-food restaurant.

Treatment plans for children and adolescents with OCD need to include both exposure to anxiety-provoking stimuli and instruction in response prevention. Response prevention involves stopping or blocking the rituals or avoidance behavior and removing the associated negative reinforcement, thereby extinguishing the behavior. Stopping avoidance behaviors is an essential part of any exposure treatment for anxiety disorders, of course, but children with OCD require special attention because they'll have well-established response patterns and rituals that will be resistant to change. Some cases will require relatively extreme measures such as not allowing a child to wash all day or even several days at a time.

Jason's Exposure Hierarchy (Obsessive-Compulsive Disorder) #2

All steps are to be completed without Jason washing his hands, showering, or changing his clothes. He may change his day clothes only at night unless his parents deem otherwise; he may shower once per day and wash his hands only before meals.

Jason's goal: To play without being bothered by worries about germs and dirt.
Exposure Stepladder:

1. Run around his yard.

2. Sit on the seat in the local park for five minutes.

3. Bounce a ball on the path outside.

4. Play outside on the path with his toy car for ten minutes.

5. Sit on the path and put his hands on the ground for two minutes.

6. Sit on the grass and put his hands on the ground for five minutes.

7. Wrestle with his father or mother on the grass.

8. Do handstands on the grass then eat something.

9. Take off his shoes after playing outside and then eat and drink something without washing.

10. Go to the bathroom and then eat dinner without washing.

11. Drip some urine on his pants and wear them all day.

Simon's Exposure Hierarchy (Social Phobia)

Simon's goal of increasing his social contacts during the weekends aims at increasing his activity level and decreasing his social isolation, providing opportunities for social-skills practice and realistic thinking about how other people view him. These activities will also be an effective part of treatment for his comorbid depression.

Simon's goal: To go out with his friends more on the weekends.
Exposure Stepladder:

1. Call Max to ask about some homework details.

2. Ask friends what they did on the weekend and extend the conversation by finding out something more about it.

3. Invite Max over for dinner with the family.

4. Call Sam and ask him to go to the movies.

5. Walk to Max's house to see if he is home.

6. Find out about taking tennis lessons and schedule a class.

7. Look interested when friends are talking about the weekend, and ask to be included.

8. Arrange to meet a friend at the mall to play video games.

9. Invite Sam to play tennis.

10. Talk to the new boy at the bus stop.

11. On Thursday, ask friends what they are doing over the weekend and suggest an activity to do with them.

12. Go to Fred's party and plan to talk to at least two strangers.

Exposure and Panic Disorder

While a true diagnosis of panic disorder is rare in children or adolescents, parents and children will often report episodes of anxiety involving intense physical symptoms such as shortness of breath, heart palpitations, sweating, shaking, and dizziness.

Usually, working with the child on learning to recognize the early signs of anxiety and using cognitive restructuring is sufficient to give the child a sense of confidence about being able to manage his anxiety. Similarly, parents benefit from having a strategy to help their child think realistically and stay cool. Both parents and children can be encouraged to realistically anticipate situations that may arouse anxiety and rehearse cognitive restructuring before panic sets in and the child appears unreachable by rational thought.

For some children, the distressing physical symptoms of anxiety become the object of fear because they're interpreted as signs of physical illness or loss of control. Children may therefore avoid situations where they may experience intense physiological symptoms or fear that they will be unable to escape if the symptoms do occur.

Joel worries excessively about going anywhere new. When anxious, he experiences dizziness, shortness of breath, and heart palpitations, and fears he may be having a heart attack. His doctor has checked Joel out and found him to be a healthy boy with no physical cause for his problems.

Joel's goal: To learn to cope with how his body feels when he is worried.
Exposure Stepladder:
Dizziness

1. Sit on an office chair and push yourself around twice.

2. Repeat the above for five minutes.

3. Whirl around in place for ten seconds and then stand still.

4. Repeat the above for two minutes.

5. Whirl around in the dark outside at night for two minutes.

6. Go on an easy fair ride.

7. Go on a harder one that whirls and changes direction.

Breathlessness and racing heart

1. Blow up a balloon without stopping.

2. Blow up an airbed.

3. Run up a flight of stairs.

4. Run up three flights of stairs.

5. Run around the park until completely worn out.

Hot and sweating

1. Sit down in a steamy bathroom.

2. Do some vigorous exercise on a hot day.

3. Sit in a sauna for fifteen minutes.

Exposure and Post-Traumatic Stress Disorder

Children and adolescents with a diagnosis of PTSD have to deal with realistic fears and their past trauma. However, they may also avoid many situations due to unrealistic fears, overestimating both the probability of such events occurring again and the negative consequences. As part of their treatment they can benefit from dealing with their avoidance of certain situations in a controlled and manageable way using an exposure hierarchy.

Rosie, twelve, has had bad dreams about car accidents ever since she was in an accident three years ago in which her mother was badly injured. She feels sick whenever she has to travel in a car, avoids traveling when she can, and is on edge and jumpy whenever she hears sudden noises.

Rosie's goal: To be able to travel by car.
Exposure Stepladder:

1. Look at the evening news with stories of accidents.

2. Visit a car-repair workshop.

3. Stand near a busy road and listen to traffic and brake noises.

4. Drive around the block with her father.

5. Drive in heavy traffic with her father.

6. Drive a short distance with her mother.

7. Drive with a friend's parents for five minutes near her house.

8. Drive further away from the house.

9. Drive at night with family or friend's parents.

10. Drive past the scene of the accident several times.

Motivation and Rewards

Everybody needs encouragement to do something difficult. When anxious adults engage in exposure, the motivating factor is the anticipation of improvement and a less anxious life. But children are not as good at working toward future goals. In addition, most anxious children do not initiate treatment themselves but are brought to treatment by their parents. Children are experts in avoiding unpleasant or difficult things and anxious children are more expert than most. Involving children and adolescents in an exposure program is a potentially frightening process that will cause their level of anxiety to increase, at least temporarily. We are, after all, asking the children to face situations or tasks that they have spent years avoiding. For this reason, we advocate the use of rewards to motivate the child's attempts at exposure and to reinforce courage. Children are much more likely to engage in an unpleasant activity in return for a tangible reward today than for an intangible reward some time later in life.

Deciding on Rewards

Most children will have no difficulty deciding on their rewards for achieving steps of the exposure program. However, it is important to broaden their understanding of the concept of rewards. The rewarding process should involve self-rewards and parental praise and recognition as well as tangible rewards from the parent. Sample exercise 11 encourages children to think of different ways they may be rewarded. Remind the parents, also, that rewards do not have to be material. Finally, in providing rewards, the principles of child management discussed in the previous chapter should be closely followed—you should remind parents of the issues related to delivering rewards. Most importantly, rewards need to be given in strict accordance with the agreement (an example of the child-management principle of consistency) and should be given as soon as possible after the step is completed. In future therapy sessions, when you check on homework progress with respect to the exposure hierarchy, you must check whether and when rewards were delivered. Parents who have not delivered rewards correctly need to be reminded of their importance.

Implementing Rewards

After formulating the hierarchy, the child and parents need to negotiate rewards for each step prior to beginning the exposures. Rewards should be contingent on the child making a serious attempt at the step (not necessarily succeeding). However, a lower reward should probably be negotiated for attempting the step and not succeeding, and a higher reward for successfully completing it. Children almost universally enjoy this aspect of the program and it is often a time of positive family interaction.

In our experience the child's newly acquired behaviors are quickly self-rewarding with many benefits of increased self-confidence and independence. We don't feel that children require extended periods of material rewards and rewards for small, in-between steps—those can be phased out after several weeks. Rewards for large steps or milestones should certainly be maintained throughout treatment. In addition, remind parents to maintain verbal praise and occasional social rewards to help with relapse prevention.

Self-Reward

Helping children learn to reward themselves for achievements increases their capacity for independence and encourages them to be less reliant on parents and teachers. Naturally, this is an essential ability for adolescents, but it's also important for younger children. Help teach children to praise themselves with positive self-talk about their efforts, such as "I did well" or "I tried hard," and to reward themselves with pleasant activities such as playing games or eating a favorite treat.

The actual reward is probably less important than raising the issue of when to reward. Many anxious children have high expectations of themselves, unrealistically expecting high achievement or perfection when trying anything new. This can contribute to their reluctance to begin any task. In many cases, this lack of confidence is manifested as feigned disinterest. These children are also likely to feel dysphoric because they are rarely, if ever, satisfied with their performance.

Restructuring the children's expectations of the importance of achievement and helping them develop more realistic standards is crucial. These children are

Sample Exercise 11:
Rewarding Myself

Doing good things for myself

1. _____

2. _____

3. _____

Doing fun things with my family

1. _____

2. _____

3. _____

My parents telling me

1. _____

2. _____

3. _____

My favorite things

1. _____

2. _____

3. _____

often focused on the end goal and need reminding to recognize and be happy with steps along the way. In particular, rewarding bravery, trying hard, or even just having a go at something new or difficult is important. The strategy of reversing roles (see chapter 5) is particularly useful here. What would this child say to a friend who had attempted this task? In a group setting, the other members of the group can be used to bounce ideas and discuss realistic standards. With individual clients, a useful homework assignment might be gathering information relevant to other people's standards. Producing more realistic standards in this way will increase the child's confidence in initiating activities and increase his tolerance of his perceived "failure" when things do not go perfectly. Further work in cognitive restructuring may be needed on the issues of perfectionism and need for achievement. Therapists need to be alert for these issues during the exposure process and be prepared to review and repeat the cognitive restructuring skills as necessary.

Conducting the Exposure

Before You Start

Naturally, once everything has been planned and prepared, the first step is for the child and his parents to select one or two steps of the hierarchy and make a commitment to practice. The first exposure sessions should be discussed in detail in the therapy session and, if necessary, rehearsed. Before attempting the first task, the child should establish a routine of thinking about the situation, practicing the detective-thinking skills, and noting his level of anxiety on the worry scale.

Some anxious children may need help in acquiring specific practical skills to deal with particular situations. For example, children planning to catch a bus may not have the necessary knowledge of procedures such as how to line up, how to be sure the bus line is going to the right place, or how to buy a ticket. Similarly, a child going shopping needs to know how to ask for help from a salesperson and when and how to deal with the money. In individual-treatment programs these skills can be discussed and rehearsed to improve the child's repertoire. Use parents or older siblings as coaches to demonstrate and rehearse skills in role plays and continue practice at home (see chapter 9). Of course, such rehearsals are needed only if the child lacks some very fundamental skills. Part of the exposure may involve trying various strategies and finding out what works for the child.

Fighting Fear

Children will keep a record of their achievement and success (sample exercise 12: Fighting Fear). Children often lose track of their successes, so these worksheets are an easy reminder of previous gains and are especially useful when the child hits some difficult spots. After completing the task, the level of worry should again be noted on the worksheet as an instant reinforcement for completing the step and as a demonstration of lowered anxiety levels (assuming

Sample Exercise 12: Fighting Fear

What did I do? _____

_____

Worry Scale   _____ Before   _____ After

What reward did I get? _____

What did I learn? _____

_____

- -

What did I do? _____

_____

Worry Scale   _____ Before   _____ After

What reward did I get? _____

What did I learn? _____

_____

- -

What did I do? _____

_____

Worry Scale   _____ Before   _____ After

What reward did I get? _____

What did I learn? _____

_____

anxiety did decrease). If anxiety did not decrease, the situation needs to be discussed to work out what went wrong and use this as a learning experience.

In-Session Practice

While all of the exposure can be set as homework outside of therapy sessions, some of the initial steps can be encountered during therapy times. This provides an opportunity to ensure that the child and parents are clear about the process, that the child is using the realistic-thinking strategies, and that the parents are able to help with appropriate management techniques. If you have the time and resources, consider spending one therapy session on an outing in which the child engages in some low-level exposure while you are present to provide coaching to both the child and parents. In a group situation, the whole group might go together to a place where all of the children will have the opportunity for some exposure. Shopping malls and fairgrounds usually provide ideal variety. In a situation such as this, the members of the group can be used to provide support, encouragement, and pressure for each other and to reward each other after successful attempts. If you do not have the time to accompany the family on an exposure step, some exposures for some children can be set up in the office. For example, socially anxious children can be asked to call organizations on the phone or meet your secretary or colleague. Children with separation anxiety can be asked to wait for a short period while their parents leave the building. Obsessive-compulsive children can be asked to go to the toilet without washing their hands.

The Importance of Home Practice

Regular practice between therapy sessions is a crucial part of this program. Repetition of the exposure steps reinforces learning new ways of doing things as well as the child's successes and feelings of mastery. Anxious children have often accumulated many "failure" experiences. Frequent repetition of the exposure steps is essential to overcome these well-established expectations, so you must emphasize the importance of regular practice. Do not allow the child to "finish" with a step after he has completed it only once.

Parents and adolescents also need to be encouraged to keep moving and not practice too erratically. How often a step is practiced will depend on practicalities; some tasks can be practiced daily or even more often. For example, if a child's task is to call an organization in order to reduce anxiety about using the telephone, there is no reason why the child cannot call several places per day. Other tasks, such as sleeping over at friends' houses or going on a school trip, may only be practiced infrequently. If this is the case that's fine, but other equivalent steps must be practiced in between, and effort must be put into brainstorming ways of creating the same or similar situations. For example, if a step involved going to an annual camp, there would be no way of engaging in this specific step more than once. However, the child could be encouraged to visit some distant relatives to produce similar steps.

Hopefully, across repeated practices, you will notice the child's anxiety in response to a given step decreasing. In fact, given the readiness with which anxious children engage in avoidance behavior, it is surprising that often a single practice is enough to dramatically reduce the anxiety associated with that situation. As the anxiety with one situation decreases, children will usually report finding the higher steps more possible due to a generalized confidence. Once the child has repeated a step one or more times and genuinely reports little or no anxiety, she needs to be instructed to move on to the next step. Given the strong avoidance tendencies that most anxious children show, coupled with the overprotectiveness of some parents, you'll often find that anxious children are reticent to move up the ladder. They tend to be happy staying at one level, continuing to get rewards for little effort. If this happens for too long, the therapy momentum stalls and everyone begins to lose motivation and confidence. If you find that this is happening, it's up to you to push exposure along. This is often one of the main traps for less experienced therapists—a tendency to get stuck. Nothing terrible will happen to the child if she is pushed. At the worst, if she has a failure or two, she can easily move back down the hierarchy a little.

As they gain more confidence and become used to the ideas of exposure, children and parents will encounter opportunities for spontaneous practice. This should be encouraged and rewarded. These spontaneous tasks may not be specifically related to the problem they are working on at the time, but may be one of the other problems from the Fears and Worries List or a previously unencountered event. Similarly, opportunities may arise to practice tasks from higher up the hierarchy that the child has not yet reached. If at all possible, the child should be encouraged to try these as best he can, as long as it does not seem to be too far out of reach. For example, a child who is afraid of meeting other children may be invited to a friend's birthday party. Going to a party may still be several steps above the child's current progress on the hierarchy. But invitations to birthday parties, for this child, are relatively rare. This sort of opportunity, then, would be too good to miss and the child should be strongly encouraged (and rewarded) to attend. If the situation seems very overwhelming, there may be ways of reducing the anxiety—for example, Mom could go with the child, the child may only commit to go for half an hour, and so on. But grabbing the opportunity is important. Of course, there will be times when the opportunities that arise are just too hard for the child, in which case you need to immediately take off the pressure and give permission to avoid at this stage so that the parents and child do not get into arguments. For example, a child who still shadows her mother around the house may be invited to travel with a friend's family for a one-week vacation. At this stage of therapy, this may be simply too hard for the child and the best approach would be to accept the child's position and help her (and her parents) with realistic thinking to deal with any depression or guilt she may be experiencing.

Resources

Use resources in the community, family, and school system to provide a wide range of exposure situations. Younger children will generally need direct involvement from parents and assistance from others to set up some more advanced exposure situations. Most people are willing to assist children who are learning new skills and readily understand the basic concepts involved once they are explained. Encourage grandparents and others not to be *too* helpful and to allow the child to experience some anxiety.

Teachers or school counselors may also be useful in helping to discreetly organize exposure steps in real-life settings at school. In our experience school personnel are very receptive to involvement in these programs. In some cases, however, it may be best not to involve the class teacher because the child needs to experience genuine responses to his new behaviors. In other circumstances, especially when early successes are particularly important, involvement of the class teacher to obtain a special response is invaluable. For example, a child who is afraid to ask a question in class because of a fear of making a mistake may be encouraged to ask questions as one step in the hierarchy. To ensure a success in the early stages, you might choose to involve the class teacher and ask him to praise the child regardless of the question. Later exposures should involve "mistakes" to demonstrate to the child that making mistakes is not a tragedy. In the latter instance, the teacher may not be informed at all, or may be informed that he should not make special allowances for this child's mistakes.

For example, Jessica worried about not doing well at school, although she usually did very well because of her perfectionist nature. However, in examinations she often performed below her teacher's expectations because she would "blank out" with anxiety. With the aid of the school, Jessica's hierarchy included mini tests, a practice exam, and time in the school hall that was to be used as the examination room to practice coping strategies. Jessica and her parents enlisted the help of the school in planning the hierarchy and organizing each step. Her teacher arranged a dress rehearsal with the class before the big day. (As a side note, Jessica's teacher and principal became so enthusiastic about the success of the program and the benefits to Jessica that they have incorporated it into the regular class preparation for exams for all the children.)

Watch for Subtle Avoidance and Safety Cues

People can reduce their fear through superstitions and idiosyncratic behaviors such as carrying a lucky charm or special toy, wearing certain lucky clothes, humming a song, chewing gum, or going through a particular ritual before doing something that provokes anxiety. (All these methods of avoidance are used by adults, too.) Other forms of subtle avoidance are also used to reduce anxiety—for example, children with OCD may engage in covert rituals, and children with separation fears may feel safe while carrying a mobile phone. In these cases, children may attribute their improvement and newly found confidence to the lucky charm or safety cue rather than to their own capacity to face up to the fears.

To overcome anxiety completely, the child needs to encounter the situation without the use of the protective object or ritual. This does not need to occur from the outset, but can be included in the hierarchy by placing a particular activity together with the object at one step and then repeating the same task without the safety cue on the next step. The child must be able to attribute her lack of fear to a real lack of danger, not the protective powers of the favored object.

You should discuss the use of these strategies with both children and parents because even parents may be unaware of these subtle methods of avoidance. Parents will want to be ready to counter the strategies at the time of exposure.

For example, Sally had long-standing difficulties leaving for school in the mornings. She worked hard to overcome her fears and all was going well until a surprising setback occurred. Unknown to her mother, Sally had been carrying with her a small doll that she felt brought her luck and gave her confidence. She had transferred the doll from pocket to pocket in her clothes but now she had unfortunately lost it. This loss set Sally back a few steps until her mother and therapist instigated exposure without the doll. Soon Sally had reached her earlier level of exposure and she began to realize that she really could cope without her doll.

Dealing with Difficulties

The exposure process must be flexible and responsive to the progress of the child. It is not a rigid process that must be strictly adhered to. If the child is having difficulties at a certain level, the exposure program may need to be redesigned to overcome the problem.

It Hasn't Worked in the Past

Because exposure is a commonsense technique, many parents will have attempted elements of it in the past. If it did not work, they may raise this as an argument against its efficacy. Similarly, many therapists in the field know vaguely of the benefits of exposure and will often give parents incomplete instructions in how to help their child in this manner. If this has happened and, again, it didn't work, this may further undermine parents' confidence in the value of the strategy.

If you come across this attitude, you need to stress very strongly the fact that study after study reports the value of exposure as the most important component in anxiety-management programs. It is important for the family to be motivated; exposure is not likely to work if it is not applied systematically and consistently. You need to ask the family about their previous attempts in detail. You will likely be able to identify ways in which the methods were inconsistent and haphazard. In addition, the role of exposure in the context of an overall anxiety-management program needs to be stressed. Cognitive restructuring, relaxation, or the basic principles of child management were most likely not taught to these families during their previous attempts.

Progress Is Slow or Nonexistent

The child may refuse to try the next step or may want to give up the exposure or move very slowly through the steps. First, consolidate progress so far by repeating the current step and, if necessary, the steps previously achieved. Next, you need to decide if the next step is really too difficult. If so, intermediate steps with smaller degrees of difficulty need to be added. Try repeating the realistic-thinking skills in relation to the new step. There may be unforeseen worries that this step has raised that need to be dealt with before the child can progress.

Discuss with the parents their attitude and feelings toward their child's progress. One or both of the parents may be giving the child covert messages about taking the next step. Their own anxieties about the situation may need to be dealt with: ask the parents to think realistically about the situation and what they expect their child to do. Parents sometimes disagree about what the expectations should be for their child. Some parents may be hesitant to push a child too hard and so allow avoidance of the situation. This avoidance can be blatant—such as the parents who simply allow the child not to do the step—or it may be more subtle, such as the fine line parents have to draw when deciding whether a child is too sick to go to school.

Also, children will lose interest in the exposure program if parents are not consistently rewarding them for completing a step. You may find that parents are not praising the child for their achievement or that rewards have been promised and not delivered. Some children, and even adolescents, may need the encouragement of an instant reward rather than delayed gratification through earning points.

Speeding Through

Moving too quickly through the hierarchy may mean the steps are not difficult enough. Another possibility is that a subtle form of avoidance may have occurred—did the child stay in the situation long enough for effective exposure to occur? If this is a problem, add a line to sample exercise 12 (Fighting Fear) that reads, "How long did I stay in the situation?" Remember, if the child says, "That's easy, I don't really need to do it again," you may want to ask him to try it again anyway.

Trying Too Hard

Some anxious children will be so eager to please their parents and their therapist that they will select an exposure step that is just too difficult to start with. You'll want to encourage such a child and praise her for her eagerness, but long-term success of the program requires that an easier target be selected for the initial exposure program. Although it is not a catastrophe if the child fails at an early task, early successes really help build up motivation.

The principles of learning indicate that persistence is encouraged more through the achievement of small steps and success each time. This will assist in developing a sense and experience of mastery. Children who attempt a too diffi-cult task often end up having difficulties and think, "I'm a failure." To explain this to children, use the example of a child learning to swim and the importance of trying the shallow end of the pool first. Would they recommend throwing the child into the deep end on the first lesson?

Again, speeding up an anxious child is more difficult than slowing them down.

Dealing with "Failure"

There is no real failure in exposure. Any experience can be used to learn about the person's thoughts and feelings and can help in the long run. However, there will be many occasions when children will refuse to do a task that they agreed upon or will escape the situation earlier than agreed due to excessive anxiety. If this occurs, it may reinforce their sense of worthlessness and may lead to demoralization and dejection.

Parents and the therapist need to help the child place his experience into a broader context by using his realistic thinking. The child needs to identify his thoughts about the meaning of the experience. So he didn't do the task—so what? Does this mean he will never do it? Does this mean he's a worthless per-son overall? Role reversal can help here—ask the child to imagine what he would say to a friend in the same situation.

If the task was too difficult, smaller steps can be inserted. If the child had a momentary loss of confidence, he can simply try again. The most important principle when a child fails to do the exposure is to not let him lose motivation. He needs to see it as a temporary setback and try again with renewed determination.

Progress Isn't Smooth

During the exposure process there will be some days that seem better than others and progress will not be smooth. Parents and children need to be edu-cated to understand that good and bad days are a normal part of anyone's life. Parents should act as coaches to encourage the child to do the best she can on any given day and to keep trying the next day. On bad days it may be better to repeat a step that has already been achieved rather than keep pushing a more difficult step.

Parents should be taught not to allow avoidance by excusing their child from attempting a task, but at the same time not to be overly rigid about the task if it is genuinely too difficult. Allow them to have the discretion to change the task at the last minute and offer a lower reward, but remind them that the child must attempt at least some task or even a part of the set task to maintain his confidence.

Rewarding attempts and good tries as well as success at achieving the step will encourage persistence and increase tolerance of perceived failure.

Worried Sick

Most parents and therapists would agree that anxious children and adolescents wrote the book when it comes to excuses and explanations about why they can't do something. A common, and sometimes the most difficult, problem for parents to deal with is complaints of illness at times of stress. Headaches, stomachaches, and "feeling sick" are difficult to deal with if parents are not sure of the cause or if various family members have different views about the reason for the complaints.

Consultation with the family doctor and a physical review may be necessary to exclude organic problems. This is important if there is disagreement between the parents over the cause of the complaints and what is the most appropriate way to manage them. You should work with the doctor to devise a treatment plan and rationale that will provide a consistent approach to the child and parents by all professionals involved.

Once everyone agrees that the sickness is a result of anxiety and does not reflect an organic cause, the parents need to inform the child that though they are sympathetic to the sickness they will not allow the symptoms to increase avoidance. Similarly, where a child's symptoms seem to command a great deal of attention, parents need to learn to provide a brief word of sympathy and understanding and then ignore the symptoms. Children need to agree that physical symptoms make activity more difficult, but not impossible. They need to learn to tackle various activities despite their symptoms.

These issues will need the involvement and agreement of all the adults involved in the child's care. This can include the school teacher and school nurse as well as all family members. You'll need to spend some time with parents alone to agree on a plan of management that everyone will follow.

In families with a history of physical illness, there may be anxieties about disease that need to be dealt with first. Parents may need to work through their anxieties about this issue with you. They need to think realistically regarding their concerns about their child's health and the realistic consequences of both encouraging the child to challenge her fears and of allowing the avoidance to continue and perhaps worsen.

Devaluing Success

Some anxious children may react to success by playing down their achievement and denying the level of difficulty involved or denying that they actually managed to do something they previously found anxiety provoking. These children may be reacting to a pressure either internalized or perceived from parents to succeed at higher levels next time. Minimizing their successes is a way of coping with anticipated demands of higher performance in the next task. These avoidance strategies can be difficult to deal with because many parents insist that they never pressure their child.

One approach may be to ask the child to try deliberately failing at a task to experience the noncatastrophic consequences of not performing brilliantly.

For example, Jessica had been playing soccer for two years. Earlier in the season she had had a very good day when she scored two goals. Everyone in the family had been very excited at her success, but she began to play down her achievement by calling the goals a "fluke." Jessica had recently missed a few matches with tummy upsets and both her parents were concerned that she was feeling too much pressure, perhaps because her father was coaching the team.

Jessica and her mother made a plan for her to mess up at soccer practice—to make some deliberate mistakes such as accidentally kicking the ball to the wrong person, missing the ball when she went to kick it, and deliberately missing a goal. She also practiced cognitive restructuring of her fears about making mistakes and the need for perfection. This and the exposure plan were sufficient to help Jessica enjoy the game again.

Drugs and Alcohol

Experimentation with alcohol and other drugs is part of most adolescent cultures. In some cases, anxious adolescents will have discovered that they can reduce their anxiety levels by drinking or taking drugs. During assessment and ongoing treatment, discuss the role drugs may play in ameliorating symptoms of anxiety or depression. This is particularly relevant for adolescents with social phobia and adolescents with comorbid anxiety and externalizing disorders where alcohol use and abuse may be an especially common strategy. (Examples of the latter include conduct disorder and attention deficit hyperactivity disorder.)

Increasing the adolescent's awareness of how she may be using alcohol or marijuana as an avoidance strategy when faced with anxiety at parties or attending school is necessary before progress can be made in an exposure program. The adolescent may be reluctant to risk decreasing her use and tolerating the increases in anxiety levels. If this is the case, incorporating drug and alcohol-free exposures into the hierarchy will be important. As with the use of safety objects, it is essential that the adolescent attributes successes to her own abilities rather than to the substance. Teaching other coping strategies such as relaxation training (chapter 5) may also be helpful.

For example, during the course of Simon's treatment, a disturbing fact emerged. Simon admitted that he was beginning to use alcohol more and more to help combat his anxiety. It began when he went to his first school dance only last year. He was absolutely terrified of going but, due to a combination of peer pressure and pride, he decided he had to go. When he arrived, he sat with some of the other boys outside smoking and pretending it was uncool to look too eager. Eventually, one of the boys produced some cheap whiskey and Simon had a try. After that, he got into the habit of having a few drinks whenever he went out anywhere. Lately, he had begun to drink before he met up with anyone at school and even at family gatherings.

One of Simon's early exposure tasks involved going to a party. At the next session, Simon sheepishly admitted that he had had a couple of drinks to "steady his nerves." The therapist praised Simon for going to the party and completing such a difficult task. She then also spent some time pointing out to

Simon how drinking would interfere with his learning that he could cope. As part of his treatment plan, Simon agreed to reduce his drinking to allow himself to experience and deal with his anxiety. He continued his exposure program and made sure that he performed small steps so that he did not feel the need to use alcohol.

Planning Ahead

Parents of anxious children can be one step ahead of potential difficulties by being aware of their child's triggers. Younger anxious children are often unaware of the buildup of their anxiety levels and can be taken by surprise by a rapid escalation of their arousal levels. They quickly become agitated, distressed, and beyond reason. When faced with this behavior, parents may become frustrated at not being able to talk sense to the child or may become overwhelmed by their child's distress and their own helpless feelings.

Planning ahead is important for both children and their parents. Helping parents plan ahead and predict potentially difficult times and their response to the child will help them feel more competent in assisting their child. The child can rehearse cognitive restructuring steps relevant to the anticipated worry and plan other coping strategies.

For example, Sally always waited anxiously for her father to come home from work. Dad was usually home by six in the evening but Sally started worrying at about half past five, sure her father had crashed the car. She would become very distressed, and at times cry and scream that her father was dead. She would often call her father's office to check that he had left for home. Her mother had two smaller children and was usually very busy at this time of day. Her therapist encouraged her to help Sally by reminding her to rehearse her detective-thinking steps at five o'clock, well before her father was due home. She also planned to change her evening routine and prepare the meal in advance so she felt less rushed and had more time to reward Sally for nonanxious behavior by playing a game with her and the other children.

Chapter 9

Social Skills Training

Anxious children will have varying competence in social skills. Some may have adequate social skills but are either too anxious to make use of them or believe themselves to be poorly skilled. Other children, due partly to their lack of experience, may not be equipped with the skills to deal with social situations. Some anxious children will be quite competent in social situations and will not require this component of the program.

The following training has been designed for children with a skills deficit as well as children whose anxiety hinders them from performing adequately in social settings. You may need to conduct an assessment of the child's social skills in order to determine the degree of intervention needed and, more specifically, to help you determine which particular skills the child needs to develop and in which situations the difficulties occur. For example, ask the parents about the child's interactions in social situations with focus on specific difficulties such as use of eye contact, posture, voice quality, and conversational skills, and support this information from the parent using a behavioral assessment of the child. For example, the child could be given a series of role plays or interaction tasks (such as meeting another child) that are videotaped or directly observed. This has the advantage of providing you with objective information and can also be used for later feedback with the child. If an additional behavioral assessment is not possible, similar information can often be gathered from the child's interaction with you during the initial interview. For more detailed information on assessment of children's social skills, see Spence (1995).

You will need to be sensitive to cultural differences in the expression of social skills; you'll need to take cultural factors into account in assessing the child's deficits as well as when you teach specific skills. Input from the child's parents as to what is considered appropriate behavior within their culture will be important in this regard. Finally, you will need to adapt the training depending on the age of the child.

Having adequate social skills becomes even more important for children as they enter adolescence and are faced with more social pressures than ever before. Adolescents begin to spend less time at home and more time with peer groups. They may also be required to attend job interviews, give presentations, or interact with others in a workplace setting. Having poor social skills will prove a great disadvantage, so in our treatment plan social skills training is an essential component of the program.

There are three basic skill areas that will be covered in this chapter and that form the basis of social skills training:

- body-language skills such as eye contact, posture, and facial expression

- voice-quality skills such as tone, volume, pitch, rate, and clarity

- conversational skills such as greetings and introductions and initiating and holding conversations

More advanced skills, such as assertiveness and dealing with teasing and bullying, will be dealt with in chapter 10. You will not necessarily have to cover all of these areas with every child, as the child's competence level in different areas will vary. Following your assessment of the child's skills, the program can be tailored to the needs of the child.

The basic skills are taught in a three-step process: instruction, behavior rehearsal and feedback, and practice.

Instruction

The first step in social skills training is instruction. At the end of the instruction section, the child should be able to recognize the appropriate use of each of the three basic skill areas listed above. He should also be able to recognize when these skills are not being used correctly.

The skills are taught in a variety of ways: through education, discussion, brainstorming, and modeling (video modeling, therapist modeling, or modeling by a competent group member or sibling). Video modeling (video footage can be taken from movies or educational programs) is our preferred method of demonstration, if it is available. Providing video footage of children the same age as your client using the skills correctly will allow the child to adopt the new skills more quickly. You could also organize children from the local school or drama club to act out scenarios that can be taped on video. This would enable the videos to be more congruent with the child's culture. Ideally, the video footage shows both the correct and incorrect use of the skill.

To begin with, you will need to introduce the skill to the child, outlining the importance of the skill. Target only one or two skills at a time, so as not to confuse or overload the child. If video footage is not available, you will need to demonstrate the skills to the child yourself. Of course, in a group situation, a child who is competent in a particular skill can model it to the others. Each of the skill areas are discussed in this chapter, and sample ideas for demonstrating the skills to the child are provided. For each of the skills, the child should be aware of how the skills are used *incorrectly* as well as correctly.

In demonstrating these skills you will need the child to participate in some of the demonstrations. You may want to write down a short script for the child to read so that he does not have to be concerned about giving the right response. Encourage the child to focus on you because he'll be practicing the skill later.

Parents of younger children need to be aware of the skills their child is learning, and can be given instructions on each of the skills in the same way the child is instructed. This can be done simultaneously with the child or in a separate session. Informed parents can assist their child in learning these skills by modeling the appropriate behaviors at home as well as praising the child when he uses the skills appropriately.

Behavior Rehearsal and Feedback

After instruction in the skills, the child then rehearses a variety of scenarios in order to feel comfortable with the skills before using them. Rehearsal improves the child's skill level and gives her further opportunity to face situations that may cause her social anxiety, enabling her to feel less anxious in these situations. In a group setting, the children are able to practice together and the role plays can more closely parallel the child's reality. If a group setting is not available, another option is to encourage the child's sibling closest in age to come along to the therapy session and take part in the role plays.

The role plays can also be videotaped to provide the children with feedback on the progress of their skills. Some children may actually be performing the skills quite well but may perceive their performance as poor, so using videos to aid with feedback will allow these children to gain a more accurate picture of their performance. In a group setting, the other children can also provide feedback to the child. When you give feedback, gently point out to the child the areas that need continued practice. Be sure to also point out the areas in which she was successful. In a group setting you will need to provide the children with guidelines for giving feedback. You may want to set a rule about giving feedback, such as each child has to report two positive behaviors and one behavior that needs improvement.

Practice

The final step in social skills training is to set tasks for the child to complete as part of her practice. This can be incorporated into the graded-exposure tasks the child has been completing in earlier sections of the program. The child is set tasks where she can practice the skills in real-life situations such as at the local shopping center or at school. This may also involve practicing role plays at home with parents or siblings.

Children and their parents set a series of tasks they will tackle. The tasks should involve entering a social situation and using the skills they have learned in the program. (Again, examples for each of the skill areas are provided below.) Practice needs to be tailored to the specific needs of the child—you'll need to make sure the tasks are not too easy but are not unachievable.

As with the practice tasks throughout this program, the child should receive a reward for successful completion. Encourage parents to also praise and reward their child whenever they use the skills outside of their practice, because this will increase the likelihood of the child continuing to use these skills. Praise needs to incorporate specific feedback: for example, "I was pleased with the way you looked me in the eye when you asked me that question," rather than "Good work." (See chapter 7 for a more detailed discussion on giving praise and rewards.)

Monitoring whether the child is using the skills appropriately during the week may be difficult, particularly when the child is at school, but we recommend that parents of younger children monitor their child's practice and give them feedback on their skill development as much as possible. Parents of adolescents should be encouraged to be involved in the practice in a way that is satisfactory to the adolescent. For example, they may simply discuss with the adolescent successes and difficulties she has experienced with the skills. The decision regarding how much parental monitoring the adolescent should have during practice depends on her maturity and independence. However, the level of parental monitoring should also be titrated by the parents' general degree of involvement with the adolescent. For example, if the parents are very involved in her life and therapy has focused on increasing her independence, she may be encouraged to monitor the practice on her own or with a friend. In other words, developing the adolescent's independence may be more important than close monitoring of her skills. Naturally, any parental involvement with adolescents' practice should be decided in full consultation with the child.

Body Language Skills

Instruction

Eye Contact

Begin each of these segments by demonstrating the power of each skill firsthand. For example, you might begin by role-playing three scenarios with the child. During the first role play, start a conversation with the child without using eye contact. You may want to begin the conversation with a question such as, "What did you do over the weekend?" Following the role play, ask the child to comment on his experience of talking to someone who kept looking away or staring at the ground. Did he find it easy to listen to the person? Would he like to talk to this person again? Did he think the person was interested in talking to him? During the second scenario, continue the conversation using too much eye contact. Again, encourage the child to talk about his experience during the interaction. Finally, demonstrate appropriate eye contact while continuing the conversation, and again ask the child about his experience of the interaction.

You can use this role play to explain to the child what eye contact is and how it can be used to communicate different messages. The following points should be covered:

- Giving eye contact means looking the person in the eye when you are talking to him.

- Eye contact projects the message that you are interested in what the other person has to say and that you are listening.

- Eye contact allows you to receive the messages the speaker is communicating through her facial expressions.

- Looking away during conversation communicates to the other person that you are not interested or are bored and not listening.

- Too much eye contact can be off-putting and can make the other person feel uncomfortable.

Posture

Similarly, in discussing posture, you'll want to directly demonstrate the points through the use of role play, magazines, or video. For example, with adolescents who have some experience in the workplace, you may ask them to play the role of an employer looking for a new employee. The employer is going to interview three people for the job. You can act out the three interviewees, each time demonstrating a different type of posture—stiff and nervous, slouched and morose, and confident. A similar role play can be done with younger children, using the scenario of a new kid walking up to a group of kids on the playground. Use this role play to explain to the child what posture is and how it can be used to communicate different messages. The following points should be covered:

- Posture is the way in which you position your body.

- Your posture differs depending on the situation you are in.

- Your posture differs depending on what you are feeling.

- Slouching your shoulders and hanging your head during conversation may give the impression that you are not interested.

- Keeping your head down when you talk makes it difficult for the other person to hear you.

- Fidgeting may give the impression that you are bored or nervous.

- Standing too straight and stiff makes you look stressed and awkward.

- Standing or sitting in a relaxed but upright posture during conversation will give the impression that you are interested and attentive.

Facial Expressions

Once again, begin by demonstrating to the child how the use of inappropriate or minimal facial expression can make communication unpleasant or awkward. You might, for example, describe to the child an exciting movie while first holding a deadpan expression and then again using animated expression. Explain to the child what facial expressions are and how they can be used to communicate different messages. The following points should be covered:

- Facial expressions let people know what you are feeling.

- A smile indicates you are pleased or happy. In conversation a smile may indicate that you are interested in what the other person has to say and that you are enjoying the conversation.

- Sometimes when people are nervous, they smile or laugh too much. This can be off-putting for the other person.

- A blank look or a frown may demonstrate that you are bored, sad, or angry.

- A flat or expressionless face is uninteresting and likely to lose the listener's attention.

Behavior Rehearsal and Feedback

The next step involves getting the child to practice the skills that have been covered while receiving feedback. Any role plays that require the child to use the requisite skills can be used. Below are a few that we have had success with.

The Conversation Game (Younger Children and Adolescents)

The idea is for children to engage in short bursts of conversation while using the best possible body language skills. In order to reduce any pressure from poor conversational skills (which are dealt with later in the chapter), prompt the child with cue cards. On each card, print a different question that could be asked during the conversation: What hobbies do you have? What foods do you like? Where do you live? What is your favorite music? When is your birthday? In a group setting, have the children break into pairs. If you are working individually, the child can pair up with you or the child's sibling can be recruited for the game. The child's task is to engage his partner in conversation for a thirty-second period. As he converses, he has to use good eye contact, good posture, and a friendly facial expression. You may want to include a scoring system in which each partner scores the performance of the other person (a sample score card is given below). A reward should be given when the child scores full points. These role plays can also be videotaped and played back to the child so that he can monitor his progress. Point out to the child the skills that he has used well during the game. Continue practicing this game until the skills have been mastered.

Sample Exercise 13: Body Language Score Card

	Head held up	Good eye contact	Stood up straight	Friendly facial expression	Hands relaxed	Total score
Game 1	+	-	-	+	+	3
Game 2	+	+	-	+	+	4
Game 3	+	-	+	+	+	4
Game 4	+	+	+	+	+	5 ... reward!

Statue Game (Younger Children)

You will need a tape player or radio for this game, which is best executed in a group setting. The children walk around the room while the music is playing. As soon as the music stops, you call out a situation and the children have to think of an appropriate posture. For example, you might call out, "At home watching television on a hot day," "Talking to the principal," "Meeting a person your age for the first time," or "Talking to a friend." For each of these scenarios the children have to strike a pose. The trick is to stand very still in the appropriate pose, because if anyone moves they are out of the game. The winner of the game is the last person to get out.

The Job Interview (Adolescents)

This is another exercise involving behavioral rehearsal for a job interview, but this time the adolescent plays the interviewee. As the interviewee, he has to practice using his body language to show you, the employer, that he is interested, friendly, and relaxed. Again, you might wish to give the child a brief script to reduce the pressure on the content of the interview. Video is very useful to provide feedback.

Stare-off

This is a fun game for younger children who have a lot of difficulties with eye contact. This is best done in threes: two players and an adjudicator. The idea of the game is to see how long the child can stare at different parts of her partner's face without looking away. The first person to look away loses the round. The child with the most points at the end of the five rounds wins the game. The third person acts as an adjudicator to see who looks away first. If the children last longer than two minutes, both players receive a point. Children can also repeat each round while conversing. Children can either choose a topic to talk about or be given a topic. This exercise provides a form of exposure for children who fear eye contact.

Round 1: Hair

Round 2: Right ear

Round 3: Mouth

Round 4: Nose

Round 5: Eyes

Practice

Practice for the body language skills portion of the program involves practicing eye contact, good posture, and a friendly facial expression in different situations. As noted earlier, parents of younger children should be asked to monitor progress as much as possible and praise the child when they notice appropriate body language; adolescents will need to monitor their own progress, although parents may be encouraged to praise the child occasionally if the adolescent agrees.

	Steps	Reward
Step 1	Go to the local music store with Mom on Monday afternoon and ask the assistant if she has the CD I've been waiting for. I'll use a friendly facial expression, good eye contact, and good posture.	1 token
Step 2	Go to the local department store on my own on a Monday afternoon and ask the assistant for help with finding a shirt the right size. I'll use a friendly facial expression, good eye contact, and good posture.	1 token
Step 3	Go to the supermarket on my own on Saturday and ask the assistant where I can find the tomato sauce. I'll use a friendly facial expression, good eye contact, and good posture.	1 token

For example, Simon's social skills practice has been incorporated into his exposure program. Simon is not only facing a fear he has been avoiding but is also practicing his body language skills. Whenever Simon goes to the store, he makes sure his mother is with him so that she can do the buying and the inquiring. Over the past few weeks Simon has been practicing asking the shopkeeper for help and has managed to ask the shopkeeper for help. This week he has to practice asking the shopkeeper for help but this time using the skills he has learned about body language. To make the task easier the first time he tries this, Simon picks a time and day when the store will not be as crowded and he picks a store that he is more familiar with to make him feel more comfortable. As a reward, Simon receives one token. When he has five tokens his parents will take him to the movies.

Voice-Quality Skills

Instruction

Tone

One good method for demonstrating the role of voice tone is to record audio segments of voice-overs using tones that express different emotions. (Audio rather than video is necessary for this exercise so that the child cannot simply use body language as a cue.) You can either record your own voice or use recordings of other people, such as newscasters or television actors. The child should guess the feelings that are being expressed in each of the samples. Include a recording of someone talking in a monotonous tone, because this is the most likely problem for anxious children.

This exercise will allow you to explain to the child the role of voice tone in communication and to point out some of her possible problems. The following points should be covered:

- Tone refers to the way the pitch or sound of your voice varies to express different emotions.

- The tone of your voice also refers to the accent you place on different words.

- A serious tone is used to convey a serious message. A lighthearted tone can be used to tell a funny story.

- When people speak with a monotonous tone, they sound uninteresting and lose people's attention.

Volume and Rate

You can demonstrate volume and rate of speech using the cue cards from the Conversation Game. This time, the child should ask you the questions and, as you answer each, you can vary the rate and volume of your voice. Ask the child to explain how he felt when listening to you and whether he would like to talk with you further. This exercise can lead to a description of the importance of volume and rate of speech. The following points should be covered:

- Volume refers to how loudly or softly you speak.

- Rate refers to how quickly or slowly you speak.

- Sometimes people speak so softly they cannot be heard at all, which makes people lose interest.

- Speaking too quickly makes it difficult for the other person to understand what you are saying, which also makes people lose interest.

- Speaking too slowly may bore the other person.

Clarity

Role-play an example of mumbling during speech and then counterbalance this with an example of speech that is clear and easy to understand. You can do this with either video, audio, or a live demonstration. Ask the child to report how she felt while listening to you when you mumbled and when you did not mumble. You may need to challenge the notion with some children, particularly adolescents, that mumbling is a "cool" way to converse.

Clarity is an important aspect to cover when teaching a child voice-quality skills because some children, especially those with little confidence, tend to mumble when they speak. The following points should be covered:

- Clarity refers to how easily your speech can be understood.

- When you mumble, other people have a hard time listening to you and understanding what you are trying to say.

- Speaking clearly means sounding out all of the words you are speaking and remembering to finish the ends of your words.

Behavior Rehearsal and Feedback

Here are a few exercises and games to allow children to practice their voice-quality skills.

In the Movies (Younger Children and Adolescents)

This exercise focuses primarily on tone. The child is encouraged to pretend he is an actor in a movie. He can write the script himself or you can provide the scripts. In a group setting, the scripts can involve more than one character. The scripts should allow the child to express different emotions, including anger, sadness, happiness, and excitement. The following scenarios can be used as a guide.

Anger: Your brother or sister has borrowed one of your favorite toys without asking and has broken it. You have an argument with your sibling.

Sadness/Disappointment: You have been trying out for a part in the school play and your teacher has just told you that you didn't get the part. You talk to one of your friends about it.

Excitement: It is the night before your birthday. The next day you and your friends are going to a theme park for your birthday party. You are talking to one of your friends on the phone.

Happiness/Contentment: You have just finished working on a project that took a long time (such as building a sand castle or finishing a computer game). You are really pleased with the end product. You go show your mom or dad.

The child reads out the script using an appropriate tone of voice. He may either stand up or sit down, and does not have to include body language with the rehearsal because this exercise is designed to practice tone only. (As an additional exercise, this game can be repeated—after this version is mastered—using body language and other voice-quality skills.)

Tape the performance and play back the recording to the child, providing feedback about both the positives and negatives of his performance.

Hobby Talk

This exercise is designed to allow children to discover a tone they can use in everyday conversation. They can practice this by telling you about one of their favorite hobbies. You will need to tape the child talking so that she can hear how she sounds. Look out for tones that are too monotonous. Listen to the tape with the child and provide feedback on the tone. You may need to repeat this several times until the child has developed a tone suitable for everyday conversation.

Tale Time

This exercise is designed to practice volume, rate, clarity, and tone. The child needs to find a volume, rate, and clarity that is suitable to use in everyday conversation. For younger children, encourage them to bring in their favorite book from home to read out loud in front of you. The child can pick a segment of roughly three minutes' length. For adolescents, encourage them to write a three-minute speech about any topic. If this task is too difficult, they could bring in an article from their favorite magazine or a favorite scene from a book or play of roughly three minutes' length.

The child is instructed to give the reading without mumbling or speaking too quickly or too softly. This may take a bit of practice. Repeat the task after providing the child with feedback on her progress.

The Conversation Game

Once again, the conversation game used earlier can be used to practice voice-quality skills. The child alternates either answering or asking questions from the cue cards. This time the child has to concentrate on speaking clearly and not too quickly or too softly. Again, tape the game and play it back to the child, giving him feedback on his performance. The same scoring system can be used again.

Practice

The child should be required to practice using a conversational tone, a steady pace, and a clear, loud voice in different situations. Tasks can be set for practicing these skills at school, on outings with friends or relatives, while shopping, or simply at home. Remember to make the tasks clear and specific for the child, making sure the parents reward the child for completing the homework.

For example, Jessica's voice is usually as quiet as a mouse and people have a hard time hearing her. She also mumbles when she speaks. So, Jessica has started working on speaking clearly and using a loud voice. Her father and her school teacher have planned for her practice task to be carried out during school time. Each week in Jessica's class, the teacher asks one of the children to read out loud several pages of the book the class is reading. This week it is Jessica's turn. She is not happy about speaking in front of the class, but the teacher has given her the pages in advance and so she has several days to practice at home. Jessica's task is to read the pages once a day to her father. He listens to the reading and provides feedback on the tone, volume, rate, and clarity of her speech. Finally, she is to read the pages in front of the class. The teacher will monitor Jessica's tone, volume, rate, and clarity. If Jessica is able to read to the class in a loud voice and without mumbling, she is rewarded—she'll get to go swimming at the beach during the weekend with her father and one of her friends.

Conversational Skills

Conversational skills are usually the poorest feature of anxious children's social skills and will require the most work. In many cases the child is aware of the skills, but is simply too anxious to use them. Practice is valuable both to learn new information and as an exposure exercise.

Instruction

Greetings and Introductions

In reviewing and adding to the child's greeting and introduction skills, the following points should be covered:

- When greeting someone you know, it is polite to say the person's name: "Hi, Sam!"

- When saying hello or good-bye, remember to use the body language and voice-quality skills that you have learned, such as eye contact, a clear and loud voice, a smile, and a friendly tone.

- When saying hello to someone, people will often also add, "How are you?" or "How're things?"

- When you are meeting someone for the first time, you may need to introduce yourself: "Hi, my name is Simon."

- If you are in a situation where your friends do not know each other, you will need to introduce them to each other.

Using video examples or role plays, demonstrate the above information using the following scenarios: greeting a friend in the school playground, meeting someone for the first time, running into an adult that you know, having to introduce yourself, having to introduce your friends.

Initiating and Holding Conversations

Some children may find this step far more difficult than the previous skills. To begin with, encourage the child to write a list of things she looks for in a friend, including things a person could say or do that would make the child want to talk to them. The list might include: a smiling face, a good listener, sounds friendly, talks about things that I am interested in, shows interest in me. Point out to the child that these qualities are probably ones that other children might also appreciate in a friend. The session can then be built around the points the children raise. The notion can be introduced as "learning how to be friendly." Make sure the following points are addressed:

- One of the best ways to initiate a conversation is to ask the other person questions. The best questions to use are open-ended: "What sports do you like?" rather than, "Do you like football?"

- When you are getting to know someone, ask them questions about themselves, such as what they like to do in their spare time, what music they like, where they live or go to school, or where they go for holidays.

- When initiating a conversation with someone that you know, you might ask them questions about what they did over the weekend, how their sports practice is going, or their opinion about a band that you like.

- When someone is talking, let the person know you are listening by making noises such as "mmmm," "uh-huh," "aahhh," "oh," and so on. This is particularly important on the phone when the other person does not have access to your body language.

- During a conversation, stick to the topic and make sure you do not wander off it as this can be tedious and distracting for the other person. (Note: If the child is having difficulties initiating or developing conversations, this point may be best left out as it may discourage the child from talking at all. Instead, encouraging the child to think of many topics to talk about may be useful.)

- Try to take turns during a conversation so that you do not just talk about yourself or the other person does not spend the whole conversation talking about himself. Taking turns also means waiting until the other person has finished speaking before you begin to speak. Let the other person finish what he was going to say.

- Try not to give one word answers, as it may give the other person the impression that you do not want to talk to her. Try to think of other things to say about the topic.

- Sometimes you may need to interrupt someone in the middle of a conversation to give them a message. The easiest way to do this is to wait for a natural break in the conversation, excuse yourself for interrupting, and then deliver your message.

- Remember: during conversations, use your body language and voice-quality skills (eye contact, speaking in a clear and loud voice, not speaking too slowly or too fast, friendly posture, a smile, and a friendly tone).

As you address each of these points, give the child a demonstration of the appropriate use of the skill as well as inappropriate use of the skill, and ask the child what it felt like to him or what he thought of the demonstration. In addition, you may also need to address the child's unrealistic beliefs about the situation. For example, the child may hold the belief that the other person he is going to talk to will think he is boring or will not really want to talk to him. Return to cognitive restructuring and challenge the thoughts the child is having about the situation, gathering evidence about what is more likely to happen in the situation (chapter 5).

Behavior Rehearsal and Feedback

The following exercises and games have been designed to allow the child to practice conversational skills.

Conversation Brainstorm

Encourage the child to brainstorm different ways of starting a conversation. Ask the child to think of how the conversation would differ if she was meeting the person for the first time versus someone she knew very well.

Movie Scriptwriter (Adolescents)

Have the child write a script of two people meeting each other for the first time. The script should be an interaction that lasts at least three minutes, and should include instructions about the person's body language and voice quality. If you are working in a group, the children might want to work in pairs. Once the script is written, the child can then act it out with either you, another group member, or a sibling. The performance should be videotaped and feedback should be given. (In a group setting, the observers can give feedback on the performance.)

The Scenario Game

The following is a series of scenarios in which the child can practice her conversational skills. The child reads the scenario and is given five minutes to decide what she is going to say and do in the situation. After five minutes, she has to act out the scenario using her conversational skills.

- The school teacher asks you to do an errand with a child in another class that you do not know very well. You have to walk over to the office together.

- The friends you usually hang out with at school are away on an excursion. At lunchtime, you notice kids from another class playing a really fun game. You go up to them and ask to join.

- You are shopping with your mom and dad when you see one of your friends from school.

- You are out with your friends and you see one of your parent's friends. They say hello to you.

- Your mom has some friends over and they are talking in the living room. The phone rings and someone asks to speak to your mom. When you go into the living room, your mother is in the middle of a long conversation with her friends. You have to interrupt the conversation politely to tell your mother she is wanted on the telephone.

- You go to the local park with two friends from school. When you get there, some of the kids who live down the street are already playing in the park. Your school friends want to join them. You join and introduce your school friends.

- You are at school and your teacher asks you to take the new student up to the office to get some paperwork. You try to get to know this new student on the way.

- (Adolescents only) You go to a party and sit next to someone who you do not know. You introduce yourself and start up a conversation.

- (Adolescents only) There is a girl at school who you really like and want to ask out on a date. You would like to go and see a band with her that you know she loves, so you go up to her after school and ask her.

Provide feedback after each scenario (using video, if it's available). The child may need to practice the scenarios a few times to feel comfortable in the situation. If difficulties are experienced, go back to the basics of the skills, reminding the child of the important points. Again, model an appropriate way to respond in the situation and then encourage the child to repeat the scenario. For each scenario, work through any unrealistic thoughts the child may have. Challenge these thoughts and gather evidence for what is more likely to happen.

The Trouble Spot Game

Encourage the child to think of times when she has experienced difficulties in conversation. Discuss with her what happened at that time and brainstorm alternate ways to deal with the situation if it happened again. Role-play the situation with the child, using the skills she has learned, to produce a more satisfying result. For very reticent children, try brainstorming together a list of topics that might be interesting to talk about in lots of different conversations. The child might then be encouraged to write these down and memorize them.

Introductions (Younger Children)

This game is designed for a group. The children should be sitting in a circle. The first person in the circle has to introduce herself by saying her first name and an adjective that starts with the same letter as the name: "My name is Joyous Jessica." The next person in the group has to introduce himself as well as the people before him: "My name is Sporty Simon and this is Joyous Jessica. This is Sneaky Sally and this is Jumpy Jason." The last person in the circle has to introduce everybody in the group. When each of the group members has had a turn, you may want to go around the group again, giving everyone the opportunity to introduce the whole group.

The Job Interview (Adolescents)

This exercise requires the adolescent to play the role of a person at a job interview. As the interviewee, the adolescent has to tell the employer about himself. This might include hobbies, things he is good at, and what he is hoping to do when he leaves school. You might need to prompt the adolescent by giving ideas about what to talk about or by asking specific questions. The adolescent needs to remember all the basic skills for this exercise (body language, voice quality, and conversational skills). Again, use a video to record the performance. The adolescent can continue to improve the performance until he is satisfied with the skills.

Practice

The child should be required to act out in real life one or more of the scenarios that have been rehearsed during the treatment session. She may be required to talk to someone she does not know very well at school or introduce herself to someone. She may be encouraged to go to a party or to start a new after-school or weekend activity where she will meet new people. Some of the situations may be harder to coordinate, so the practice may need to be set over a few weeks to allow situations to arise naturally. Ask the child to keep track of incidental successes as well as the successes during planned practice.

For example, Sally has not attended ballet classes for some time because she has not been able to separate from her mother. She has now spent several weeks working on her exposure program and is finally able to spend time away from her mother. Sally feels she is ready to go to ballet lessons. During her treatment sessions she has been practicing introducing herself and making conversation with people she does not know. Going to ballet class is a good place for her to practice these skills, so her task is to introduce herself to one person and find out a little bit about them during the first week of ballet. She has to report back to her mother when the lesson is over and tell her the name of the child she spoke to and what she found out. Before class, Sally practices with her mother what she is planning to say. That week, Sally makes two new friends by approaching two girls who looked friendly, introducing herself, and starting up a conversation. Sally felt very proud and congratulated herself for doing so well. To reward her efforts, her Mom took her for an ice cream after the next class.

Dealing with Difficulties

Lack of Improvement

You may find that despite training in the practice of social skills, the child does not make the expected improvement. There may be several reasons for this lack of progress. The child's anxiety may not have been fully dealt with yet and so may be interfering with her ability to use the skills appropriately. In other words, the child may not actually lack skills (she may be able to use the skills in therapy sessions), but her performance of the skills may be reduced by anxiety. If this is the case, time and continued practice will likely be all that is needed for the child to become more at ease in using the skills; no additional specific skills training will be needed. However, you may want to include additional social exposure tasks to speed up reduction of the child's anxiety.

On the other hand, the lack of improvement may be due to comorbid conditions, such as prodromal psychosis, autism, or Aspberger's syndrome, in which social skills deficits are a major part. If this is the case, the deficits will need considerably more work and improvements will be slow. You may need to accept that, in such cases, improvements may remain limited.

Chapter 10

Assertiveness

Assertiveness Training

Being assertive is a way of behaving and thinking in any situation in which a child needs to express feelings, ask for something, or say no to something. An assertive child or adolescent will recognize and reveal to others what she thinks, feels, and wants in a situation while respecting the needs of other people. She will be able to communicate with others openly, directly, and clearly, and be active in pursuing what she wants rather than acting passive and feeling helpless. She may learn to accept her limitations and those of the situation and be aware that she cannot always win.

To become assertive, a child or adolescent needs to develop an understanding of his feelings and his rights in a given situation. The child needs to act in a way that shows he expects to be treated with respect and that at the same time he will treat other people's needs with respect. The more a child is able to stand up for himself appropriately and act in a manner that shows self-respect, the higher his self-esteem will be.

Children and adolescents who have difficulty acting assertively may need training in social and communication skills to learn what to say in different situations and how to speak and act in a way that lets others clearly know what the message is. Children who do not have these communication skills may often feel misunderstood or feel that people are ignoring them if they relate in a passive way. If they tend to approach situations from an aggressive stance they may not realize that a request that they intend to be reasonable comes across to others as aggressive and intimidating.

Anxious children may have difficulty being appropriately assertive for a different reason. In our experience, many anxious children, especially those with social phobia or generalized anxiety disorder, experience excessive worry about the consequences of assertive actions. This worry often centers around a fear that they may be disliked or rejected if they stand up for themselves. Both children and adolescents may also have difficulty relating appropriately with adults such as school teachers or other authority figures, fearing that the adult may become angry or irritated with their requests. In these cases, treatment will need to include cognitive restructuring to enable the child to evaluate the real risks of using assertive behavior, and exposure to allow the child to test out in real life the consequences of behaving assertively.

Various possibilities will need to be considered when you assess children to determine whether their difficulties arise from avoidance of assertive behavior due to unrealistic fears or from lack of communication skills. Different children will need different combinations of training in new ways of behaving and thinking. Your assessment will also need to determine the pervasiveness of their difficulty with assertiveness. Therefore, you should question the parents and child about the child's ability to act assertively in a wide variety of situations. Much of the assessment of assertive skills will be similar to that for the assessment of social skills described in chapter 9. For detailed information on the assessment of assertive skills, see Spence (1995).

Some children may seem to have no difficulties in putting across their point of view with parents, siblings, or close friends. However, at school or in the playground, they may complain of unfairness or being pushed around, teased, or bullied. Other children may find being assertive difficult in all situations.

Teaching children and adolescents skills in assertive behavior will involve both anxiety management and communication and social skills. An overall program includes:

- understanding the link between acting passively and negative feelings

- recognizing personal rights and responsibilities toward the rights of others

- learning the difference between assertive, passive, and aggressive behavior

- developing skills in nonverbal assertive behavior

- developing skills in verbal assertive behavior

- using cognitive restructuring to reduce fears about the negative consequences of being assertive

- using exposure to practice assertive responses in different situations

- learning to choose when to be assertive and when other social skills are needed, because being assertive may not always be appropriate or safe

Teaching these concepts to children and adolescents can be done in individual sessions or as part of a group-treatment program. Clearly, the group situation provides an ideal setting for role play and practice. Children who are more assertive can help others by modeling and suggesting different responses. However, individual therapy is also appropriate for this training—the therapist can take on the role of the group.

Assertiveness training, especially for younger children, begins with your making sure the child understands the link between passivity and negative feelings. Try to review situations in which the child has not acted assertively. If he lacks some insight, perhaps enlist the help of the parent. Hypothetical situations may also be useful. Ask the child to recall how he felt at those times when he was not able to stand up for himself. This allows the opportunity to explore what outcome the child would have preferred and what difference such an outcome would have made to his feelings. This discussion will allow you to introduce to the child the concept of assertiveness and the principles of what you will be teaching.

Next, you'll need to discuss with children the appropriateness of being assertive in different situations. Most importantly, the child needs to realize that being assertive is not a license to suddenly force her demands onto everyone in all situations. In addition, there may be times when swallowing pride and retreating is better and safer than being assertive. This is especially true in the situation of bullying (discussed later in the chapter) but is also very relevant in situations of domestic violence. Children who are in violent or potentially violent situations need to be warned very carefully that being assertive is not the best strategy when they may be at risk of physical injury. Assertiveness can often inflame a situation, especially when it is unexpected and a marked change from previous behavior. (Of course, being assertive may be an appropriate way to defuse an emerging potentially violent situation. However, this decision needs to be made on an individual basis and should not be taught in a blanket way to children who may not realize when it is safe to be assertive and when not. If you suspect that your client may be in potentially abusive situations, the usual notifications and precautions need to be taken.) In short, try to convey to children that assertiveness is a wonderful skill, but it must be used with responsibility and care.

Rights and Responsibilities

Ask the child to suggest some ways that she would like to be treated that are fair and safe. Ask her to imagine she is making new laws for the world about how people should treat each other. Putting these rights and rules into a list that the child can take home and add to is also useful. A discussion can be prompted by asking for brief examples of times she has been treated unfairly. The aim here is not to resolve the unfair event or suggest solutions but to elicit the basic rights that were transgressed.

The child needs to realize that rights involve a balance between personal satisfaction and the satisfaction and needs of others. Children who are somewhat aggressive versus children who are somewhat anxious may have different problems with balance. Aggressive children may need to be helped in developing some empathy by being asked about the other person in a situation. For example, a child may say that he should have a right to play the drums whenever he wants. You might use this opportunity to ask him about the other people in the house and in the street. The use of role reversal, which children should be familiar with by now, might help. Such children need to realize that rights are not absolute and may vary with time, place, and circumstances.

Anxious children are not very likely to overdemand their rights. In contrast to aggressive children, they are more likely to fail to come up with rights because of excessive empathy and concern for others. The use of role reversal can help in these cases as well. Try to get these children to realize that they are as important as others and that if they believe that others have certain rights, then surely those rights extend to them too.

Express the rights in a positive form and ensure that they are appropriate for the child's developmental stage and culture. For example, it would be unreasonable for a young child to expect to have the right to make all the decisions about himself. Some children will be familiar with some of these concepts from personal-development and personal-safety programs in school.

My rights:

I have a right to be safe and not be hurt.

I have a right to ask for what I need.

I have a right to make mistakes.

I have a right to say no to anything that seems unsafe or that I feel is wrong.

I have a right to do what I enjoy.

My responsibilities:

I should treat others with respect.

I should not do anything to harm or hurt others.

I should try to respect the needs and wishes of other people.

I should allow others to make mistakes.

I should allow other people to have ideas and opinions different from my own.

Teaching Children Nonverbal Assertive Behavior

Anxious children will often indicate their uncertainty with passive body language that contradicts the message they would like to convey. This discrepancy will give a mixed and confusing message to others, markedly decreasing the probability of the anxious children achieving what they wanted. In order to become more assertive, children need to learn the appropriate nonverbal behaviors.

The main techniques for helping children act more assertively are the basic social skills that were covered in chapter 9. The main difference here is in the focus of outcome. In the previous chapter, we discussed social skills from the perspective of helping children become more liked and more able to communicate. In this phase of treatment, these same skills can be taught with the aim of getting the message across clearly and with an air of confidence and sureness.

Again, each skill should be discussed and practiced, and the different messages provided by different demonstrations of the skill should be illustrated. For example, the role of eye contact could be discussed again, this time with a role play focusing on the way eye contact communicates passiveness, aggression, or assertiveness.

The concepts of nonverbal assertive behavior should be rehearsed with role plays and real-life situations. Young children can be introduced to three characters who demonstrate different response styles—Passive Pat (head down, slumped over, body turned away, no eye contact), Aggro Alex (threatening body posture, staring, aggressive gestures), and Assertive Andy (standing tall, head up, appropriate eye contact). Discuss with young children how each of these characters would behave nonverbally, paying special attention to the characters' body posture and eye contact. You can role-play the nonverbal behavior of the three characters yourself, or, in a group setting, other members can play a part. (Be sure to repeat the role plays to ensure that all group members have an opportunity to participate.) Videotaping the practice and viewing it together for feedback is very effective.

Activities for Groups

Younger children enjoy the Guess Who I Am game: children take turns pulling one of the character's names out of the hat and acting out the part. The other members guess whether they are Passive Pat, Aggro Alex, or Assertive Andy. Older children often enjoy playing the part of favorite TV characters to demonstrate the typical characteristics of assertive, aggressive, and passive behavior.

Ask the children to focus on how their bodies felt when playing the various roles. How did they feel inside? What differences did they notice when they became Assertive Andy? What did others in the group think when they saw Passive Pat and Aggro Alex? Emphasize the point that feelings inside can change when you change the way you stand and look at people.

Practice

Ask the child to try out some of these assertive body-language skills at home between sessions by practicing in front of the mirror and with family members, and remind her to notice how she feels inside after trying each one.

The following quick checklist can be useful to remind children of the skills, and they may wish to rate themselves, or have their family rate them, on how well they are using their nonverbal assertive skills.

- Look at the eyes.
- Stand up straight.
- Show a confident, friendly face.
- Keep your hands relaxed.
- Have a clear, loud voice.

Teaching Children to Speak Assertively

Adult programs that teach assertive language usually include strategies such as the use of empathy, "I" statements, and cause-and-effect statements. Most of these strategies are not developmentally appropriate for children, however. A typical child would not use a sentence such as, "When you speak to me that way, it makes me feel uncomfortable and I would prefer it if you used a softer tone." Not only would teaching children such language be difficult, it would cause great ridicule among their peers. The fact is, most children and adolescents do use relatively abrupt and sometimes aggressive language when they want their way and this is quite acceptable among various age groups.

Therefore, in teaching a child assertive language, this developmental difference needs to be kept in mind and assertive language should deal with only a few simple principles. Older adolescents can be taught some of the principles of adult assertive language because of their need to deal with, and be assertive with, adults.

Hints for Children

- Keep it simple. Children need to be taught that if they want their message to get across clearly, it needs to be simple and to the point. Long-winded explanations will lose the listener and make the speaker appear weak and uncertain. Often, children will need instruction in how to say a simple "No" to things they feel are wrong or unsafe. They need to do it in a way that clearly indicates how they feel, while using appropriate and consistent body and voice cues.

- Give a reason. Using hypothetical situations, you can get children to imagine whether they would be more likely to do something for someone who simply demanded it, or for someone who provided a reason. For example, "Can I borrow your CD?" is much more likely to get a response if a reason is attached: "Can I borrow your CD—I really love that band."

   That said, it is also important to acknowledge that sometimes reasons can leave a person vulnerable. Older adolescents may need to discuss the situations in which *not* providing a reason is more sensible, such as cases in which the reason acknowledges a vulnerability: "I would really like to be invited to your party" is much better than, "I would really like to be invited to your party because I have nothing to do on Saturday."

- Don't blame. People are very unlikely to help or to change their behavior if they think they are being blamed and abused. Again, getting the child to realize this message through the use of a role play or hypothetical situation can be very helpful. When explaining this to children, use dialogue such as, "Can I have my pencil please?" versus "You always take my pencils!" Younger children may have more difficulty with this principle since they are more likely to insist on retribution. Encourage them to think about the difference between retribution and getting what they want.

Practice

Teach the concepts of assertive, passive, and aggressive language using the vignettes below or others from the child's experience. Role-play each scene using passive, aggressive, and assertive response styles. For younger children, you may want to stick with the same characters—Passive Pat, Aggro Alex, and Assertive Andy.

You may need to take the part of each character initially. Later, involve the child in acting out the scenes. Use scripts if necessary to get children started. Again, the use of feedback from the group leader and other group members and use of videos is important to help the child develop their skills and improve their abilities. Remind children to use their nonverbal assertive skills while trying the assertive language.

While discussing and role-playing these scenes, it may become appropriate to remind the child that being assertive will not always provide a positive result. Given that assertiveness involves acknowledging the other person's rights, there may be times when the other person exercises their rights and refuses to comply. Take the opportunity to remind children of this possibility and to discuss the use of cognitive restructuring to deal with any disappointment or anger.

Jim's New Car

Jim is playing outside his house with a new remote-control car he has just been given for his birthday. Ben, the boy from around the block, wants to play with it too. Jim agrees and lets him have a turn but then becomes worried that Ben seems to be playing roughly with his new car. Jim wants to keep playing with Ben but does not want his car to be damaged. What would Passive Pat, Aggro Alex, and Assertive Andy say?

Maria's Ice Cream

Maria bought an ice cream at the corner shop but when she unwraps it outside the shop, she finds it partly melted. She wants to return it to the shop and get another one that is frozen solid. What would Passive Pat, Aggro Alex, and Assertive Andy say?

Carla and Sarah

Carla has worked hard on her history project and is proud of the good job she has done on her research and illustrations. The day before it is due to be handed in, Sarah, a girl from her group, asks Carla if she can see what she has done to get some ideas. Sarah has asked this before and Carla knows she copied a lot of her project last time. Carla does not want to let Sarah see her project but is worried that Sarah may get angry with her. What would the three characters say?

Steve Lends Money

Tim asked Steve to lend him some money last week as he had forgotten his lunch. He promised to bring it in to repay Steve the next day. A week has gone by and Steve has not had his money returned. He sees Tim buying himself a drink and feels it is unfair that Tim has not paid him back yet. What would the three characters say?

Dealing with Aggression

Books on assertiveness usually include sections detailing various "tricks" for getting your way in the face of aggressive or uncooperative people. We do not generally advocate most of these procedures for children. However, it is a fact of life that children are often nasty or unpleasant to each other. We therefore discuss one or two simple diffusion techniques with some of the children who go through our programs. These techniques can easily result in escalated aggression, so we generally do not cover them with children who may abuse them—those who are aggressive, those with especially poor skills, or those who do not seem to catch on easily. Nevertheless, for the right child, these skills can be of value in the face of difficulties.

Broken-Record Method

The broken-record approach is a way to deal with people who just do not seem to get the message no matter how clear the first assertive message has been. Children should be taught that they can use this technique when their request seems to have been ignored. However, it should not be used to beat into submission a person who is voicing his own rights in a responsible manner. Most importantly, children need to be taught not to use this technique if they are in danger of being physically injured. For example, in the event of bullying or threatened violence, the broken-record technique is not advised as it may escalate the situation. The technique involves simply reasserting the basic message in a clear and persistent manner. The voice should remain calm and steady.

Sandy loaned her new CD to Jason so he could tape it. He has not returned it although Sandy asked him to a week ago.

Sandy: Jason, I want that CD back from you.

Jason: Well, I haven't finished with it yet. I haven't got a tape.

Sandy: I want my CD back. I want to listen to it.

Jason: Mom's going to get a tape over the weekend. I'll bring it back then.

Sandy: Jason, you have had it for ages. I want my CD back tomorrow.

Jason: Well, I haven't had a chance to listen to all of it yet and I really like it.

Sandy:	I want my CD back tomorrow. Please bring it to school tomorrow.
Jason:	Okay, can I borrow it next week?
Sandy:	Thanks. I will lend it to you when I have finished with it.

Fogging

Fogging is a technique to deal with criticism, baiting, and teasing by deflecting the attack. Fogging involves verbally agreeing with a critical remark or a part of the criticism in a neutral and calm manner. The child does not have to fight back or defend himself. This approach takes the attacker by surprise and gives him nothing to bounce off of to escalate a fight. Bullies will often use baiting or teasing comments to stir up a less assertive or more vulnerable child and enjoy seeing him grow upset. Teaching children how to seemingly accept the criticism dispassionately gives them a method of removing the emotion from the situation and reduces the chance of escalation.

The main risk from fogging is a loss of self-esteem by having a child who simply seems to give in to an aggressor. You'll need to help the child distinguish between their verbal comments as a type of weapon against attack and their own beliefs. Reminding them to use their detective thinking (cognitive restructuring) is also important. Fogging could also, at times, inflame a situation if it seems to be used as a type of taunting or sarcasm, so the child must be instructed to use a completely neutral tone. In addition, she needs to keep a close check on the other person's body language and drop the technique if it does not seem to be working.

Fogging is done either by specifically agreeing with part or all of the comment, or by making a general remark such as "You could be right about that" or "That might be so."

Sofia:	You failed the math test. You must be the dumbest person in class.
Susie:	Yes, I did fail the test this week.
Jerry:	You look weird in those jeans, no one wears those anymore.
Nigel:	You could be right, there aren't many of these jeans around.

Practice

Role-play assertive responses to one or more of the examples given below, then use feedback to modify the responses, and repeat the role play. Ask the child for a situation he would like to handle differently and rehearse some assertive responses to real-life situations. Encourage the child to try out the different techniques he has been learning and discuss which ones seem to work best in different situations.

Here are some problem situations for younger children:

1. The girl sitting next to Lisa at school asks to borrow her new pencils to finish a drawing at home.

2. Ben is at the shopping center with his friends and they dare him to steal something from a shop.

3. Jurgen is being teased by a boy at school about his new glasses. The bully accuses him of looking stupid.

4. Some of the girls in Paola's group are teasing and whispering about one of the other girls. Paola doesn't want to be part of it.

Here are some problem situations for adolescents:

1. Two of Sally's friends are planning to skip school on Friday to go into the city. They ask Sally to come with them.

2. Austin is standing outside the movies with his girlfriend when two boys his age tell him he is too ugly for his girlfriend.

3. Dan's friend Mike is visiting him while his parents are out. Mike wants to drink some of Dan's father's beer.

Once the various skills and techniques for acting assertively have been taught and practiced in session, the child needs to begin to implement these strategies in real life. For those children who simply lacked a few skills or perhaps had been overly aggressive, this step simply involves identifying some real-life situations in which they have failed to be assertive in the past and making a commitment to approaching them differently in the future. The child should keep a record of the situations in which she attempted to be assertive and what the outcome was.

Most anxious children will have a history of avoiding assertiveness due to fears of being rejected or disliked. By now, you should have spent some time applying cognitive-restructuring strategies to these worries. In the next stage, the act of being unassertive needs to be thought of as a type of avoidance (the child is avoiding assertive actions). The child should begin to address these fears using the principles of exposure. Use her experiences to list a range of difficult situations she would like to handle in a more assertive way. These situations can be used to draw up a hierarchy of difficult situations (chapter 8) to allow gradual exposure to increasingly difficult situations. In a group program, you can use the group to brainstorm possible solutions and approaches to the problem. The child should then select the first step (or more) of the hierarchy. Each task should be role-played in the session first so that the child can be provided with feedback and modification. Homework should involve a commitment to practice. When necessary (especially in the initial stages), parents need to be included to provide rewards. Eventually, however, successful assertiveness will provide its own rewards.

Bullying and Teasing

While many terms have been used to describe the intimidation and abuse of one person by another, we will use two terms here: teasing and bullying. We use the term "teasing" to refer to a low-level, primarily verbal abuse of a child by another. The term "bullying" is used to refer to more intense—usually physical—and potentially dangerous abuse.

Bullying and teasing are very real problems for many children. Only in recent years have these problems begun to be addressed in a systematic way in schools. There have now been major advances in the development of antibullying strategies in schools, though past attitudes (that bullying is a part of growing up and children just have to learn to deal with it) still prevail in many schools and households. Hopefully, the introduction of school-bullying programs will have a long-term effect in changing the attitudes of students and staff, making schools become aware and responsive to the problems associated with bullying and reducing the level of violence in schools.

Bullying and teasing can take place in all schools regardless of age range, type of school, location, and culture or composition of intake. However, teachers may be unaware that bullying is occurring, leaving students to believe that they are abnormal or at fault because no one is doing anything about it. Compounding the problem, parents are also usually unaware of the bullying or teasing because for several reasons children are often reluctant to open up. First, there is a school code and a culture of scorn for the child who tattles on other children. Many children are threatened by bullies and fear the consequences of informing on their tormentors. Also, most victims—particularly of long-term bullying—at least partially believe that they are to blame for the bullying because they deserve it. From the child's perspective, he is affected not only by what is actually happening to him but also by the threats and fears of what may happen. The bully does not have to be present for a child to be anxious or distressed.

Children are also affected by seeing bullying occur, whether it consists of another child being physically intimidated or hit or the teasing of name calling or being excluded from a group. Children can also worry about bullying or aggressive behavior they witness a teacher give to another student.

Most children will encounter teasing and bullying behavior as they grow up, and even later in the workplace. Whether the child actually becomes a victim depends on a number of factors. The child's initial response is a major determinant; bullies intimidate and harass for a number of reasons, the most common being that they think the victim cannot overpower them and they can get away with it.

The teasing and bullying may be occurring in more than one situation—at school, with friends, and during after-school activities. This may lead the child to think that there is something wrong with him and that he is at fault. Of course bullying is completely unacceptable behavior, but it is worth considering whether the child may be responding in a way that is maintaining the teasing or bullying. Becoming distressed and crying, and/or losing control by shouting or attacking can often reinforce the bully's behavior.

Some anxious children may be particularly at risk for being teased and bullied, because shy and less socially confident children may lack the personal skills and confidence to react in a way that will deflect the bullying behavior. Teaching assertive skills can help, but should not be a substitute for concerted and effective action by parents and the school in dealing with and stopping the intimidatory and violent behavior of bullies. This should be the first priority of any parent, teacher, or therapist who becomes aware of bullying behavior.

Dealing with Teasing and Bullying

Children experiencing teasing need to learn strategies to cope more effectively with the situation and need help considering how they can behave differently. Assertive children may still be teased occasionally, but the attack is less likely to be continued because their response deflects it. The assertive child will deal with the problem with minimal emotion, depriving the bully of his reward.

Children who can deal with minor teasing by themselves will feel a sense of satisfaction at their developing skills and their achievement. The first step is to discuss the teasing with the child to get an idea of the extent and parameters of the problem. Where there appears to be even the slightest risk of physical danger, these strategies should not be used due to the risk of inflaming the situation. Instead, the school needs to be consulted to develop a more holistic approach to the situation in consultation with the parents and child. The strategies listed below are therefore only applicable in the case of teasing, not bullying. The strategies can be helpful in reducing the likelihood and extent of teasing and are essentially extensions of the assertiveness skills that were covered earlier in this chapter.

Ignoring

This is probably the most effective method of dealing with teasing and aggressive gestures. Children are likely to have been advised in the past to ignore the attacker, but this may not have worked due to inconsistent or brief ignoring. Explain to the child that ignoring will work but will not necessarily be quick. In addition, they need to be warned that the teasing may escalate temporarily as the teaser attempts to get a response by methods that have had spectacular results before. The ignoring must be consistent and persistent in order to be effective.

Because of the difficulty of ignoring the teasing in the face of escalation, help the child develop skills through role play. In a group situation, the other members of the group can take turns playing the teaser. In the individual situation, you will need to be the teaser. Ask the child for as much information regarding the usual teasing scenario as possible to make the role play more realistic. Here are the tips for ignoring that you should cover with the child:

- Do not make eye contact with the teaser or give any indication that you have noticed his presence.

- Imagine a shield around you that provides protection against the verbal onslaught. Visualize the color and shape of the shield and imagine the teasing comments bouncing back off the shield without reaching or harming you.

- Practice a bored or disdainful look to help you control any outward signs of distress.

- Imagine the bully with something embarrassing happening to him such as forgetting to put his pants on or developing large warts all over his face.

Cognitive-restructuring practice may help reduce the impact of the teasing, and repeated role-play practice will help desensitize the child to the effects of the teasing and build confidence in his ability to cope.

Being Assertive

The assertiveness skills of saying no and fogging can also be useful when children are being teased. Fogging, in particular, can be a valuable strategy since it provides the victim with something concrete to say and do. In contrast, the broken-record technique is not usually appropriate as it may escalate the situation, triggering a more physical response.

Have the child practice the application of saying no and fogging through role plays. Give direct feedback via video or reflected feedback from others to shape the child's ability. Cover the following points:

- Use assertive and confident nonverbal behavior.

- State your points clearly and simply.

- With fogging, acknowledge the teaser's argument partially or entirely in a noncommittal fashion.

- Try not to look angry or frightened and do not buy into the argument.

Use of Humor

While ignoring and fogging are the most effective strategies for eliminating or at least reducing chronic teasing, the use of these strategies may come at the price of reduced self-esteem and reduced credibility in the eyes of others. In some situations, especially where teasing is not chronic and where there is little risk of violence, it may be important for an anxious child to learn to defend herself. This is especially the case in situations of verbal abuse and put-downs.

Ideally, the best response is a humorous reply that puts the other person on the defensive. This requires practice and confidence. When the teasing itself has been expressed in the form of humor and the child is viewed as taking the comments too seriously and becoming too angry over the remarks, she will be accused of lacking a sense of humor. Being able to come back with a humorous response lets the other person know that she was not distressed by the comments and is not intimidated.

The child will need to practice the use of humor. Humor dries up in situations of fear, so the need for repeated practice must be emphasized. The use of cognitive restructuring is also important to put the comments into perspective and reduce the reaction to them. Children are often reassured by learning a few stock remarks that they can use at times when they are unable to think of anything else to say. You may wish to set a homework exercise for the child: watch several sitcoms and write down the best one-liners. However, the child needs to understand that if the humor is itself a put-down, the situation could easily escalate to violence. The humor must be funny and deflecting without being derogatory toward the attacker.

Dealing with Difficulties

Fears about the Consequences of Being Assertive

One of the major problems for anxious children is not so much not understanding how to be assertive, but fear of the negative consequences. Because of excessive and unrealistic fears about these perceived negative consequences, the child may adopt a passive approach and avoid dealing with some situations or people.

Anxious children may fear they will be unpopular or will be rejected by friends if they stand up for themselves. They may be concerned that adults and other children will get angry or see them as being demanding or selfish.

If the child is socially anxious, he will likely deny the strength of his feeling and will avoid negative appraisal by shrugging off the impact of an event. In these cases, accept the child's argument that the event has little impact, but point out that it may still be somewhat better to be assertive. For example, "I know you don't really mind, but wouldn't it be better for you if . . ." or "I know it's not a big issue for you, but wouldn't you feel happier if . . ."

When dealing with passive children of this type, you'll need to remind them of the value of detective thinking (cognitive restructuring) and help them apply their strategies to assertiveness situations before you go on to teach assertiveness skills. Ask the child to identify the thoughts or beliefs underlying her passiveness, then challenge her fears with the cognitive restructuring questions she has learned and check for evidence to back up the underlying beliefs. Remember to use role reversal with the child as well.

Physical Abnormalities

Some anxious children may get teased due to an obvious physical feature such as protruding ears or obesity. In many such cases, the strategies described earlier should work to reduce the teasing. However, in some cases, the teasing will be so marked due to the obviously "different" appearance of the child that she will be unable to deal with it. It cannot be stressed enough that the input and cooperation of the school will be invaluable in all cases of teasing and especially bullying. In cases of marked teasing, a meeting will need to be arranged between the appropriate school personnel (school psychologist or principal), the parents, and yourself to plan an effective strategy. Most schools are very open to such approaches.

Chapter 11

Closure

If you have followed this program closely with your client, you have hopefully noticed marked changes. As discussed in the opening chapter, we view anxiety as a part of the child's basic makeup, so you and your clients need to be realistic about the extent of expected change. A highly anxious child is unlikely to become the bravest or most outspoken of the group. But anxious children can and do make dramatic changes and you should certainly expect your client to reach a point at which anxiety is no longer a major determinant or a markedly interfering factor in her life. Again, our outcome research has indicated that over 75 percent of the children who complete the program no longer meet the clinical diagnosis of an anxiety disorder at the end of treatment and for at least one year beyond. (Of course, any additional or comorbid disorders may still remain after successful treatment for the anxiety. In this case, you will need to either refer or commence treatment for these additional disorders.)

The Closing Session(s)

In the final session(s), you will need to make sure that your client and her family leave with an appreciation of the gains she has made and of the need to maintain those gains. The first aim of the final session is to review the techniques that have been covered and discuss with the family the specific strategies that seem to have been most beneficial. Many people think that these changes just "happened" for some sort of random reason. You need to encourage both child and parents to view any changes as being due to the work that they put in and the specific techniques that they practiced. Ask the child to summarize each of the techniques that he learned, ask the parents to add any others they can think of, and, finally, you should remind them of any that they missed. Discuss with the family the main principles of each technique and the ways in which they used them. In particular, get them to focus on those strategies that *they* found most useful. A good method of doing this is to provide the child and parents with a hypothetical threat situation and ask them to brainstorm how they would approach it. For example, you may ask them to imagine that the child was about to leave home to go to college and felt very nervous. How would they approach this fear? Or, what if the child was asked to give a talk at an important awards night ... how might he prepare?

Spend some time discussing treatment progress. Hopefully, you're ending treatment because the child has made good gains. However, sometimes people in therapy forget or discount how severe their anxiety was at the beginning of treatment. In this case, you may find the family perceiving less change than there really was. Pull out your notes from the initial assessment and go over these with the child and his parents. This is where the value of standardized questionnaires is apparent. If you gave some psychometric tests at the beginning of treatment, you should repeat these now (or between sessions). You can then go through the scores together with the family and point out the degree of change. Going over the parents' descriptions in the initial interview and through the child's monitoring forms from the early sessions can also be useful. Of course, it is essential to point out to the family that treatment is not over. In our research we have typically found continued gains following the end of formal therapy. You need to emphasis to your family that change has not necessarily finished just because formal sessions with you are over; they still need to continue to practice and especially to confront feared situations. Some therapists like to set a booster session four to eight weeks in the future to encourage their clients to continue practicing.

Perhaps the child has *not* made good gains. In most such cases, you would not be ending treatment but might go back to additional assessment, a renewed formulation, and perhaps a modified therapy tack. However, in some cases, the family and yourself may have decided to terminate therapy at this stage. In this case, the final session will still be very similar to the above: you'll want to point out any changes that have been made, remind the child and parents of the techniques, and encourage continued practice. Most importantly, however, you should point out your views of why you think gains have not been made, even if this proves to be quite confrontational. Even if the family does not accept your formulation immediately, there is always the possibility that it will stay with them and begin to make sense at a later point in their lives.

Finally, you'll need to briefly raise the issue of relapse. A return of anxiety can occur for several reasons. In some cases, when people stop having difficulties they become complacent and stop practicing their techniques. When this happens, anxiety can begin to creep back subtly until life gradually becomes more and more restricted again. A major life event can also bring back anxiety. In the case of anxious children, the most common cause of relapse is disharmony and breakup of the family. However, an infinite number of other events can also trigger relapse by sapping confidence, including illness in the child or family, burglary, a serious accident, death in the family, bullying, or a school failure. In all cases, relapse can be countered by simply going back to basics again and starting the program over. Point out that a relapse is not a complete failure but is often an understandable slip that can be reversed just as easily. The child needs to understand that once he has learned the skills of anxiety management, they can never be taken away. He may slip backward a bit for certain reasons, but the basic knowledge of anxiety management will always be there. Going back to basics is not an admission of defeat but a simple way of getting everything moving the right way again. Almost always, improvement will be much faster the second time around, so in a sense the child will never again really be starting from square one. The most important thing in the case of returning fear is not to become depressed or demoralized and give up altogether. As long as the family is prepared for the possibility of relapse, they should be able to tackle it.

A Brief Word about Medication

A percentage of children with anxiety disorders are on medication for their anxiety. While medications for anxiety in children are not used as commonly as they are for adults, many of the same medications are used from time to time. Benzodiazepines are prescribed much less for children than they are for adults; tricyclics and, more recently, SSRIs are more common. By the completion of the program, a child should be competent to manage her anxiety without medication. Per our discussion in chapter 1, you may have tapered off the medication toward the end of treatment and had the child complete some of the exposure exercises without medication. (If not, now is the time to suggest to parents that the child do so. Be sure to warn the family of the possibility of a temporary increase in anxiety while medication is reduced. As discussed earlier, medication reduction should be gradual.) Of course, we strongly recommend that any discussion and alteration of the medication regimen be conducted in consultation with the prescribing physician. Some physicians will not be willing to recommend reduction of medication until after the treatment plan is completed. In such cases, you should discuss a plan for possibly returning to see you for a few booster sessions around the time that medication is reduced.

A Graduation Certificate

Our practice has been to give children completing the program a certificate to mark their successful change and to congratulate them on the hard work they have done. In our group program, we finish with a small party where each child receives a certificate and is congratulated by the rest of the group. We can tell from the looks on their faces that the children really appreciate being acknowledged in this way—it is another success they can add to their portfolio.

CONGRATULATIONS

on completing the coping kids group

_____

_____

Figure 7: Congratulations Certificate

Afterword

We hope that you've found this program useful and that you have been able to use the suggestions to successfully treat one or more anxious children. If you were an experienced child therapist before beginning this treatment plan, we hope you've found at least some suggestions here to bolster your skills. If you were a relative novice, we hope that the chapters have provided you with a basic framework for the treatment of anxious children that will allow you to incorporate it into your own therapeutic style. We have always found the treatment of anxious children to be extremely rewarding. The families are generally friendly and grateful for help and the children are usually motivated and work hard. We hope that your experiences have also been positive and that this book will enable you to build your expertise in the understanding and treatment of the anxious child.

Appendix

Running Treatment
in Groups

The treatment program described in this book is designed to be used in individual therapy *or* in a group treatment setting. In our programs, most children and adolescents are treated in small groups with concurrent parent groups. Outcome evaluation of the programs has shown that this group approach is at least as effective as previous individual-treatment approaches in reducing levels of anxiety reported by children and their parents. Naturally, they are more cost effective because of the larger numbers we can treat within a given period of therapist time. Group sessions usually take an hour and a half to two hours.

Group treatment has several benefits over individual treatment for anxious children. Attending a group appears to have the effect of normalizing the problem for both the children and their parents. Children attending the group often comment that they were relieved to find that they were not the only anxious child around and that anxiety disorders are surprisingly common among children. This is especially relevant for older boys who have the social pressures of being expected to be tough and capable and not to admit being anxious, fearful, or worried. The group setting is an automatic opportunity for exposure and provides relatively nonthreatening opportunities for shy and isolated children to practice social skills and friendship development. Parents also gain considerable support and encouragement from attending the group program. The parent sessions focus on educating parents about anxiety and the skills their children are learning as well as behavior-management skills. Parents report that they gain substantial benefit from meeting other parents of anxious children, allowing them to discuss difficulties and compare notes on management skills.

Group Makeup

The number of children in a group can vary according to demand for treatment, but the program will work effectively with a minimum of four and maximum of eight children of similar ages. Ages of the children will depend on referrals, but we have found that groups of children two to three years apart in age work well. Children younger than seven may not benefit as much from group treatment. Ideally, groups should be balanced for gender. Single-sex groups have been run, but in our experience some boys find it difficult to talk about their fears in boy-only groups due to social pressures to appear capable and fearless. In mixed sex groups, be sure to ensure that both sexes have more than one representative.

Attendance

Parents and children should be encouraged to attend groups on time and regularly. This should be clearly stated before the group starts and repeated at the first session. You can reinforce this by being prepared for the group, starting on time even if not all members are there, and by having clearly defined finishing times. We have also found that making sure the therapists are in the group room ten minutes before the starting time can be rewarding for families who arrive promptly. We frequently have one or two families in a group who fail to attend one or two sessions. If a family misses a session, you should spend a brief period of time separately with them (either on the telephone or before the next session) filling them in on the missed information and making sure that they have all of the necessary paperwork. Missing one or two sessions does not seem to affect the outcome, but families who miss more than two sessions may need to be asked to wait until the next group or may need to be referred to individual treatment. Motivation would need to be seriously questioned and other issues that are likely to hinder progress may be identified in such cases.

Therapists

The group program allows for flexibility in the involvement of therapists. In our programs, usually two therapists will run the group, spending time with both children's and parents' groups. This allows one therapist to briefly assist children who may be having difficulties grasping some concepts while the other can hold the rest of the group to the tasks and activities. Anybody (parents or children) not actively involved with a therapist is able to network and develop valuable skills: the children are able to interact and develop social skills and friendships and the parents often form their own support group to discuss important issues. Alternately, depending on the therapist's experience and the group size, one therapist may work with the children and another with the parents. This format allows more time for discussion with parents who may be having management difficulties and allows the total time each week to be less.

Finally, we have run some groups with only a single therapist with no apparent decrease in effectiveness.

Younger Children

We successfully conduct programs with children as young as seven years and occasionally include children at the upper end of six. In addition, we are beginning to conduct similar programs with the parents (not the children) of temperamentally anxious four-year-olds and initial results are promising. Children seven and up are generally able to grasp the concepts of cognitive restructuring reasonably well. With children younger than seven, you may need to skip this component. Younger children will usually need greater assistance from parents to complete the program; the younger the child, the greater the required involvement from parents. Parents should be taught the basic steps and can be invited back into the group session and rehearsed in this with their children before the end of each session. The parents' role is to assist and facilitate the child's practice rather than take responsibility for the task being done or nag the child to do the homework. They may be able to provide opportunities for practice and will be able to take advantage of spontaneous situations in the latter stages of the exposure phase to encourage extra practice.

Adolescents

Adolescents present particular challenges in groups. The marked differences in developmental stages and levels of sophistication makes selection of group members important to ensure a cohesive group process. Adolescents and their parents will have very different ideas of how involved the parents should be and this should be negotiated both at the assessment stage and when forming the group. Treatment groups for this age group will function better if the parents have a separate group with limited involvement with their children. With older adolescents, it may be appropriate to hold the parent sessions on a separate day or to hold less regular information sessions about the content of the program only. In fact, adolescent anxiety management can be conducted effectively without parent involvement (Barrett et al. 1996). However, *some* brief updating of parents is beneficial. Negotiate with the adolescents which issues they feel comfortable having discussed at the parent session. In addition, adolescents should be encouraged to discuss with their parents the degree of involvement they would like with them in their program.

Parents

Parent involvement is an essential part of the treatment program for younger children (Barrett et al. 1996). In preparing for the group program, parents need to be aware that they will be active participants in their child's treatment and should attend each session.

Ideally, both parents should attend the group, but this is often not possible due to work or child-care commitments. We attempt to involve the absent parent by providing written information detailing the ideas explained in each session. We also have special evenings in which we give an overview of the program for those parents who cannot attend treatment sessions. In general, as long as the parents are encouraged to communicate regularly about the program and their child, there are few problems involved in having only one parent attend a given session.

In the case of separated or divorced parents, we see it as even more important that both parents attend the group, especially if the child spends time in both households. It is essential that the two households engage in consistent strategies, though this can be impractical if there is open conflict between the parents. There may also be legal requirements that both parents be advised of the treatment plan and agree on their child's involvement. They may wish to attend parents' evenings or may require separate information and discussion sessions to involve them in their child's progress.

During the program, parents may reveal their concerns with anxiety symptoms, a previously undiagnosed anxiety disorder, or other difficulties. Some of our parents have used the program to effectively deal with their own specific phobias, ably assisted by their children who have drawn up exposure hierarchies. For more complex issues, you might arrange additional individual sessions or refer the parent to additional therapy, because there is rarely time for discussion of these issues in group time. Extended discussion of family and marital conflict and concerns about other children have the potential to derail the parents' group session and will need to be dealt with in a separate therapy period.

Items to Keep in the Facilities

The groups will require two rooms, one large enough to contain all parents and children for the beginning and end of sessions. At least one room should contain a blackboard or large sheets of paper. Video equipment and a monitor are useful if the social skills components of the program are included. Name tags for adults and children are a useful icebreaker, as are some board games for the children. Parents enjoy access to a nearby room with the means to make tea and coffee. Stickers or candy for the children can be valuable as rewards for appropriate behavior.

Group Rules

Establishing some simple rules is an important part of forming the group and building trust. This needs to be done in the first group session and either written on a sheet of paper to be displayed at each session or copied and distributed to each group member. The group members may be able to suggest some rules themselves or with prompting from group leaders. Typical rules should include issues of safety for themselves, others, and property; confidentiality and privacy;

acceptance of others' problems; and letting everyone have a fair turn to talk. Here are some sample rules:

- We won't laugh at other people's difficulties or fears.
- We won't tell people outside the group about private matters within the group.
- We will listen when other people talk.
- Only one person talks at a time.

Warm-up Games

Warm-up games are useful for many reasons: to introduce group members to each other, for group cohesion, to develop a group identity, to assist in the development of group and interpersonal skills, and to prepare the group for the work to be done. Group games can also be used in the middle of a session to liven up a group that seems flat or inhibited. The following games have proved useful to us. The group leaders should explain the rules of the game and keep the group focused on what they are doing.

Introducing Group Members (Sessions 1 and 2)

Detective Clues: The group members split into pairs and interview each other, asking questions such as, "What is your name?" "How old are you?" "What is your favorite food?" When everyone has finished, each child introduces their partner to the rest of the group with a few facts.

Bingo: Draw up a grid of nine or twelve squares and in each write an item appropriate to the group members (likes chocolate, plays football, has a dog, has a parent who wears glasses, loves pizza). The group members' task is to mingle around the room talking to the other children to collect the names of the group members who fit the description of each square. First to finish calls out "Bingo!" This game is useful to activate group members who are nervous and shy at the first or second session.

Name Ball: Get group members to sit in a circle on the floor or around a table. The first person starts by rolling a soft ball to another, saying his name and the name of the other person: "I'm Nick, you're Tom." This continues around the circle: "I'm Tom, you're Sally . . ." Once this is started it can be played faster and another ball added for a larger group.

Games for Group Building

Crazy Machine: Make a clear space in the room and explain to the group that they are going to invent a special machine. Ask one child to start making a machinelike motion with sound effects, and then each child can join in to add another action.

Shark!: Clear a space in the room and lay sheets of newspaper on the floor. These sheets become islands. The children should walk around the room until you call "Shark!" At this point, they all have to reach an island and stand with no feet in the "water." When you call "Back in the water" they start swimming around again. Take away pieces of paper or make the islands smaller and smaller. The group has to squeeze onto the islands to escape the shark until it has eaten enough.

Pictionary: Adolescents enjoy this board game.

Reporting on Progress during the Week

Round the Group: Quickly go around the group, asking each person the same question. (Best thing that happened this week? Best reward? Hardest thing to do?) Encourage short answers rather than anecdotes to keep the momentum building around the group. This game works well to end a session (What did you learn today? What will you remember from this?).

Chance: Ask the children to throw a die to answer questions about what they have done during the week in terms of home practice. On even numbers they have to tell the group what they practiced; on odd numbers they can ask any group member what they have done.

Pick It: The therapist writes a number of questions on cards and places them in a box. As group members arrive they pick a card from the box. After the group starts, each member takes a turn to answer their question. The questions should be relevant to the stage of the program that the group is at. For example:

- What was the bravest thing you did this week?

- What made you the most scared and how did you cope with it?

- Who has been surprised by your bravery?

- What did you do this week that you couldn't do before?

- What was the most helpful detective thought?

- What did you do that you were proud of and how did you reward yourself?

These questions can be answered by one child or used to facilitate group discussion, drawing in other group members to compare experiences.

Final Session

As discussed in chapter 11, we like to end the group program with a celebration: a party at which we hand out certificates marking the successful completion of the program. Where there has been good group bonding, participants may wish to have a more personal farewell. Some groups may wish to exchange contact details. This should be done with parents' consent and involvement only.

About You: Have sheets of paper printed with each group member's name on top or ask each group member to draw an outline of their hand on the paper. Pass the sheets around and ask other group members to write positive comments about the person and his achievements. Parents may join in with groups of younger children.

Intensive Program

The group-treatment program designed to be implemented over nine weeks has also been modified to an intensive one-week format. This is designed to provide an opportunity for rural and isolated children and their families to access treatment. Families live in a residential facility during the week of the treatment program and are involved in a daily program. All the usual components of the treatment program are included, but families learn the strategies and conduct practice on a daily basis. Parents are able to attend a more intensive parent-skills program during the week. A sample timetable is shown below.

Over the intensive week, the children can also attend the school program within the facility between therapy sessions. Alternately, if the program is run over a school-vacation week, the children can be involved in recreational activities that also provide opportunities for exposure. Following the intensive week, the children and their families are offered continuing support and ongoing therapy through liaison with local health services and education staff.

Table 9: One-Week Intensive Program

Day 1	Day 2	Day 3	Day 4	Day 5
Welcome and introduction session. Discussion of thoughts and feelings. The nature of anxiety. Cognitive restructuring.	Review cognitive restructuring. Child management. Introduce exposure and construct hierarchies.	Review exposure and hierarchies, cognitive restructuring, and child management. Conduct in vivo exposure and discuss the results.	Conduct in vivo exposure. Discuss the use of cognitive restructuring with exposures. Training in social skills, assertiveness, and teasing as needed.	Conduct in vivo exposure. Review techniques and difficulties. Discuss ongoing practice and set goals. Graduation party.

References

Achenbach, T. M. 1991. *Manual for the child behavior checklist #4-18 and 1991 profile.* Burlington: Department of Psychiatry, University of Vermont.

Anderson, J. C., S. Williams, R. McGee, and P. A. Silva. 1987. DSM-111 disorders in preadolescent children: Prevalence in a large sample from a general population. *Archives of General Psychiatry* 44:69–76.

Andrews, G. 1996. Comorbidity in neurotic disorders: The similarities are more important than the differences. In *Current controversies in the anxiety disorders,* edited by R. M. Rapee. New York: The Guilford Press.

Barrett, P. M., M. R. Dadds, and R. M. Rapee. 1996. Family treatment of childhood anxiety: A controlled trial. *Journal of Consulting and Clinical Psychology* 64:333–342.

Barrett, P. M., R. M. Rapee, M. R. Dadds, and S. Ryan. 1996. Family enhancement of cognitive style in anxious and aggressive children. *Journal of Abnormal Child Psychology* 24:187–203.

Beck, A. T. 1976. *Cognitive therapy and the emotional disorders.* New York: New American Library.

Beidel, D. C., S. M. Turner, and T. L. Morris. 1995. A new inventory to assess childhood social anxiety and phobia: The social phobia and anxiety inventory for children. *Psychological Assessment* 7:73–79.

Bernstein, D. A., and T. D. Borkovec. 1973. *Progressive relaxation training: A manual for the helping professions.* Champaign, Ill.: Research Press.

Birmaher, B., S. Khetarpal, D. Brent, M. Cully, L. Balach, J. Kaufman, and S. McKenzie-Neer. 1997. The screen for child-anxiety-related emotional disorders (SCARED): Scale construction and psychometric characteristics. *Journal of the American Academy of Child and Adolescent Psychiatry* 36:545–553.

Borkovec, T. D., and E. Costello. 1993. Efficacy of applied relaxation and cognitive-behavioral therapy in the treatment of generalized anxiety disorder. *Journal of Consulting and Clinical Psychology* 61:611–619.

Caspi, A., G. H. Elder, Jr., and D. J. Bem. 1988. Moving away from the world: Life-course patterns of shy children. *Developmental Psychology* 24:824–831.

Caspi, A., T. E. Moffitt, D. L. Newman, and P. A. Silva. 1996. Behavioral observations at age 3 years predict adult psychiatric disorders: Longitudinal evidence from a birth cohort. *Archives of General Psychiatry* 53:1033–1039.

Chorpita, B. F., and D. H. Barlow. 1998. The development of anxiety: The role of control in the early environment. *Psychological Bulletin* 124:3–21.

Cobham, V. E., M. R. Dadds, and S. H. Spence. 1998. The role of parental anxiety in the treatment of childhood anxiety. *Journal of Consulting and Clinical Psychology* 66(6):893–905.

Eisen, A. R., and W. K. Silverman. 1993. Should I relax or change my thoughts? A preliminary examination of cognitive therapy, relaxation training, and their combination with overanxious children. *Journal of Cognitive Psychotherapy* 7:265–279.

Fergusson, D. M., J. L. Horwood, and M. T. Lynskey. 1993. Prevalence and comorbidity of DSM-111-R diagnoses in a birth cohort of 15-year-olds. *Journal of the American Academy of Child and Adolescent Psychiatry* 32(6): 1127–1134.

Foa, E. B., M. E. Franklin, K. J. Perry, and J. D. Herbert. 1996. Cognitive biases in social phobia. *Journal of Abnormal Psychology* 105:433–439.

Foa, E. B., and R. J. McNally. 1996. Mechanisms of change in exposure therapy. In *Current controversies in the anxiety disorders*, edited by R. M. Rapee. New York: Guilford Press.

Hudson, J. L., and R. M. Rapee. In press. The origins of social phobia. *Behavior Modification*.

Hudson, J. L., and R. M. Rapee. 1998. Parent-child interactions and anxiety. Paper presented at the World Congress of Behavioral and Cognitive Therapies, July, Acapulco, Mexico.

Kaufman, J., B. Birmaker, D. Brent, U. Rao, and N. Ryan. 1996. Kiddie SADS—present and lifetime version (K-SADS-PL): Initial reliability and validity data. *Journal of the American Academy of Child and Adolescent Psychiatry* 36:980–988.

Kazdin, A. E., N. H. French, and A. S. Unis. 1983. Child, mother, and father evaluations of depression in psychiatric inpatient children. *Journal of Abnormal Child Psychology* 11:167–180.

Kendall, P. C. 1992. *Coping Cat Workbook*. Ardmore, PA: Workbook Publishing, Inc.

Kendall, P. C. 1994. Treating anxiety disorders in children: Results of a randomized clinical trial. *Journal of Consulting and Clinical Psychology* 62:100–110.

Kendall, P. C. 1992. *Coping Cat Workbook*. Ardmore, PA: Workbook Publishing, Inc.

Kovacs, M. 1981. Rating scales to assess depression in school-aged children. *Acta-Paedopsychiatrica* 46:305–315.

Kowalenko, N., A. Wignall, S. Kennedy, and R. Rapee. 1998. Fighting fears: The treatment of anxiety disorders in children and adolescents community clinic and rural outreach. Paper presented at Third National Conference on Child and Adolescent Mental Health, July, in Sydney, Australia.

Last, C. G., C. C. Strauss, and G. Francis. 1987. Comorbidity among childhood anxiety disorders. *The Journal of Nervous and Mental Disease* 175:726–730.

Manassis, K., and S. J. Bradley. 1994. The development of childhood anxiety disorders: Toward an integrated model. *Journal of Applied Developmental Psychology* 15:345–366.

March, J. S. 1998. *Manual for the Multidimensional Anxiety Scale for Children (MASC)*. Toronto, MultiHealth Systems.

March, J., and K. Mulle. 1998. *OCD in Children & Adolescents: A Cognitive Behavioral Treatment Manual*. New York: Guilford Press.

Meichenbaum, D. 1977. *Cognitive-behavior modification: An integrative approach*. New York: Plenum.

Ollendick, T. H. 1983. Reliability and validity of the revised fear survey schedule for children (FSSC-R). *Behaviour Research and Therapy* 21:685–692.

Phillips, S. D., and M. A. Bruch. 1988. Shyness and dysfunction in career development. *Journal of Counseling Psychology* 35:159–165.

Rapee, R. M. 1996. Improved efficiency in the treatment of childhood anxiety disorders. Paper presented at the thirtieth annual convention of the Association for the Advancement of Behavior Therapy, New York.

———. In press. The development of generalized anxiety. In *The developmental psychopathology of anxiety*, edited by M. W. Vasey and M. R. Dadds. New York: Oxford University Press.

Rapee, R. M., P. M. Barrett, M. R. Dadds, and L. Evans. 1994. Reliability of the DSM-III-R childhood anxiety disorders using structured interview: Interrater and parent-child agreement. *Journal of the American Academy of Child and Adolescent Psychiatry* 33:984–992.

Rapee, R. M., E. M. Litwin, and D. H. Barlow. 1990. Impact of life events on subjects with panic disorder and on comparison subjects. *American Journal of Psychiatry* 147:640–644.

Rapee, R. M., and L. F. Melville. 1997. Retrospective recall of family factors in social phobia and panic disorder. *Depression and Anxiety* 5:7–11.

Rapee, R. M., and A. Szollos. 1997. Early life events in anxious children. Paper presented at the thirty-first annual convention of the Association for the Advancement of Behavior Therapy, Miami Beach, Florida.

Reynolds, C. R., and B. O. Richmond. 1978. What I think and feel: A revised measure of children's manifest anxiety. *Journal of Abnormal Child Psychology* 6:271–280.

Rosenbaum, J. F., J. Biederman, B. A. Bolduc-Murphy, S. V. Faraone, J. Chaloff, D. R. Hirshfeld, and J. Kagan. 1993. Behavioral inhibition in childhood: A risk factor for anxiety disorders. *Harvard Review of Psychiatry* 1:2–16.

Sanders, M. R., and M. R. Dadds. 1993. *Behavioral family intervention.* Needham Heights, Mass.: Allyn and Bacon.

Schniering, C. A., J. L. Hudson, and R. M. Rapee. In press. Issues in the diagnosis and assessment of anxiety disorders in children and adolescents. *Clinical Psychology Review.*

Shaffer, D., M. Schwab-Stone, P. W. Fisher, P. Cohen, J. Piacentini, M. Davies, C. K. Conners, and D. Regier. 1993. The diagnostic interview schedule for children—revised version DISC-R: Preparation, field testing, interrater reliability, and acceptability. *Journal of the American Academy of Child and Adolescent Psychiatry* 32:643–650.

Silverman, W. K., and A. M. Albano. 1996. *Manual for the anxiety disorders interview schedule for DSM-IV: Child and parent versions.* San Antonio, Tex.: Psychological Corporation.

Spence, S. 1995. Structure of anxiety symptoms among children: A confirmatory factor analytic study. *Journal of Abnormal Psychology* 106:280–297.

Spielberger, C. D. 1973. *Manual for the state-trait anxiety inventory for children.* Palo Alto, Calif.: Consulting Psychologists Press.

Strauss, C. C., C. A. Lease, A. E. Kazdin, M. K. Dulcan, and C. G. Last, 1989. Multimethod assessment of the social competence of children with anxiety disorders. *Journal of Clinical Child Psychology* 18:184–189.

Torgersen, S. 1983. Genetic factors in anxiety disorders. *Archives of General Psychiatry* 40:1085–1089.

Verhulst, F. C., J. van der Ende, R. F. Ferdinand, and M. C. Kasius. 1997. The prevalence of DSM-III-R diagnoses in a national sample of Dutch adolescents. *Archives of General Psychiatry* 54:329–336.

Wignall, A., and R. M. Rapee. 1998. Social phobia in children and adolescents: A group treatment program. Paper presented at the World Congress of Behavioural and Cognitive Therapies, Acapulco, Mexico.

Williams, S. L. 1996. Therapeutic changes in phobic behavior are mediated by changes in perceived self efficacy. In *Current controversies in the anxiety disorders,* edited by R. M. Rapee. New York: Guilford Press.

Ronald M. Rapee, Ph.D., is a professor in the Department of Psychology at Macquarie University in Sydney, Australia.

Ann Wignall, M. Psych., is a clinical psychologist with the Department of Child and Adolescent Psychiatry of Royal North Shore Hospital in Sydney.

Jennifer L. Hudson is a psychologist and graduate student in the Department of Psychology at Macquarie University in Sydney.

Carolyn A. Schniering is a psychologist and graduate student in the Department of Psychology at Macquarie University in Sydney.

Companion Guide for Parents

HELPING YOUR ANXIOUS CHILD

A Step-by-Step Guide for Parents
Step-by-step strategies that parents can use to help their children cope with anxieties and fears. By Ronald M. Rapee, Ph.D., Sue Spence, Ph.D., Vanessa Cobham, Ph.D., and Ann Wignall, M.A.   *Item HAC $12.95*

Further Professional Reading

TREATING DEPRESSED CHILDREN

Incorporates stories, games, and role playing to provide a full twelve-session course of treatment.   *Item TDC $49.95*

MANAGING CLIENT ANGER

Helps therapist understand their own anger and make constructive interventions when clients express anger toward them.   *Item MCA $49.95*

TREATING PANIC DISORDER AND AGORAPHOBIA

Psychologist Elke Zuercher-White describes a full 12-session treatment program. *Item AGOR Hardcover $44.95*

SHORTER TERM TREATMENTS FOR BORDERLINE PERSONALITY DISORDERS

Offers treatment approaches aimed toward realistic short-term goals. *Item BOPE Hardcover, $39.95*

Call **toll-free 1-800-748-6273** to order. Have your Visa or Mastercard number ready. Or send a check for the titles you want to New Harbinger Publications, 5674 Shattuck Avenue, Oakland, CA 94609. Include $3.80 for the first book and 75¢ for each additional book to cover shipping and handling. (California residents please include appropriate sales tax.) Allow four to six weeks for delivery.

Prices subject to change without notice.

Some Other New Harbinger Self-Help Titles

Virtual Addiction, $12.95
After the Breakup, $13.95
Why Can't I Be the Parent I Want to Be?, $12.95
The Secret Message of Shame, $13.95
The OCD Workbook, $18.95
Tapping Your Inner Strength, $13.95
Binge No More, $14.95
When to Forgive, $12.95
Practical Dreaming, $12.95
Healthy Baby, Toxic World, $15.95
Making Hope Happen, $14.95
I'll Take Care of You, $12.95
Survivor Guilt, $14.95
Children Changed by Trauma, $13.95
Understanding Your Child's Sexual Behavior, $12.95
The Self-Esteem Companion, $10.95
The Gay and Lesbian Self-Esteem Book, $13.95
Making the Big Move, $13.95
How to Survive and Thrive in an Empty Nest, $13.95
Living Well with a Hidden Disability, $15.95
Overcoming Repetitive Motion Injuries the Rossiter Way, $15.95
What to Tell the Kids About Your Divorce, $13.95
The Divorce Book, Second Edition, $15.95
Claiming Your Creative Self: True Stories from the Everyday Lives of Women, $15.95
Six Keys to Creating the Life You Desire, $19.95
Taking Control of TMJ, $13.95
What You Need to Know About Alzheimer's, $15.95
Winning Against Relapse: A Workbook of Action Plans for Recurring Health and Emotional Problems, $14.95
Facing 30: Women Talk About Constructing a Real Life and Other Scary Rites of Passage, $12.95
The Worry Control Workbook, $15.95
Wanting What You Have: A Self-Discovery Workbook, $18.95
When Perfect Isn't Good Enough: Strategies for Coping with Perfectionism, $13.95
Earning Your Own Respect: A Handbook of Personal Responsibility, $12.95
High on Stress: A Woman's Guide to Optimizing the Stress in Her Life, $13.95
Infidelity: A Survival Guide, $13.95
Stop Walking on Eggshells, $14.95
Consumer's Guide to Psychiatric Drugs, $16.95
The Fibromyalgia Advocate: Getting the Support You Need to Cope with Fibromyalgia and Myofascial Pain, $18.95
Healing Fear: New Approaches to Overcoming Anxiety, $16.95
Working Anger: Preventing and Resolving Conflict on the Job, $12.95
Sex Smart: How Your Childhood Shaped Your Sexual Life and What to Do About It, $14.95
You Can Free Yourself From Alcohol & Drugs, $13.95
Amongst Ourselves: A Self-Help Guide to Living with Dissociative Identity Disorder, $14.95
Healthy Living with Diabetes, $13.95
Dr. Carl Robinson's Basic Baby Care, $10.95
Better Boundries: Owning and Treasuring Your Life, $13.95
Goodbye Good Girl, $12.95
Fibromyalgia & Chronic Myofascial Pain Syndrome, $19.95
The Depression Workbook: Living With Depression and Manic Depression, $17.95
Self-Esteem, Second Edition, $13.95
Angry All the Time: An Emergency Guide to Anger Control, $12.95
When Anger Hurts, $13.95
Perimenopause, $16.95
The Relaxation & Stress Reduction Workbook, Fourth Edition, $17.95
The Anxiety & Phobia Workbook, Second Edition, $18.95
I Can't Get Over It, A Handbook for Trauma Survivors, Second Edition, $16.95
Messages: The Communication Skills Workbook, Second Edition, $15.95
Thoughts & Feelings, Second Edition, $18.95
Depression: How It Happens, How It's Healed, $14.95
The Deadly Diet, Second Edition, $14.95
The Power of Two, $15.95
Living Without Depression & Manic Depression: A Workbook for Maintaining Mood Stability, $18.95
Couple Skills: Making Your Relationship Work, $14.95
Hypnosis for Change: A Manual of Proven Techniques, Third Edition, $15.95
Letting Go of Anger: The 10 Most Common Anger Styles and What to Do About Them, $12.95
Infidelity: A Survival Guide, $13.95
When Anger Hurts Your Kids, $12.95
Don't Take It Personally, $12.95
The Addiction Workbook, $17.95
It's Not OK Anymore, $13.95
Beyond Grief: A Guide for Recovering from the Death of a Loved One, $14.95

Call **toll free, 1-800-748-6273,** or log on to our online bookstore at **www.newharbinger.com** to order. Have your Visa or Mastercard number ready. Or send a check for the titles you want to New Harbinger Publications, Inc., 5674 Shattuck Ave., Oakland, CA 94609. Include $3.80 for the first book and 75¢ for each additional book, to cover shipping and handling. (California residents please include appropriate sales tax.) Allow two to five weeks for delivery.

Prices subject to change without notice.